A MOORSIDE LAD

David James Lavisher was born in 1943 in Moorside and grew up in the village. His teenage years were spent in the fleshpots of Oldham, in its decadent and exciting heyday of the late 1950s to the early 1960s (wherein lies another story). Other leisure time in his youth was taken up playing football in Oldham's Amateur Football Leagues and he was a motor-cyclist for a few years until he became fed up with being wet-through most of the time.

For most of his adult life David was employed by Oldham M.B.C. and worked in the Environmental Health Department – a job that he enjoyed.

For the past 25 years he has written poetry with some success. In the late 1970s and early 1980s his poems were published regularly in *Lancashire Life* magazine, the *Oldham Weekend Chronicle* – often, the *Huddersfield Examiner* – intermittently since then. Many others appeared in national magazines and various anthologies.

He has been a prizewinner in poetry competitions over the years – the most recent being in the Lancashire Authors' Association – of which he is a member – winning their 'Poetry in Standard English 2001' competition and was pleased to win their 'Writer of the Year Award 2001'.

David attended the Blue Coat School in Oldham and is a member of the ex-pupils' Old Blues Association. He lives in Slaithwaite, West Yorkshire, with his wife Sylvia. They like to travel abroad, visiting friends in America and driving round Europe enjoying historical cities and the different cultures. At home, he writes and does a spot of fishing when time permits. He has two further books in progress – one a fiction novel in its early stages and the other a sequel to *A Moorside Lad*, telling of his youthful experiences in Oldham during the Rock and Roll years.

A Moorside Lad

Growing up and having fun 1948–1955

Jade Publishing Limited

5 Leefields Close, Uppermill, Oldham, Lancashire OL3 6LA

This first impression published by Jade Publishing Limited 2002.

© D. J. Lavisher 2002
 All rights reserved.

ISBN 1–900734–22–2 A Moorside Lad – Growing up and having fun
1948–1955.

Printed in Great Britain

Typeset by Baz, Littleborough, Lancashire OL15 8RH

British Library Cataloguing in Publication Data
Lavisher, David J.
A Moorside Lad – Growing up and having fun 1948–1955.
1. Lavisher, David J. – Childhood and youth 2. Moorside (England) –
Social life and customs
 I. Title
942.7'393'0854

ISBN 1–900734–22–2

Dedication.
To Sylvia

CONTENTS

ILLUSTRATIONS

There are 9 plates between pages 56 and 57. All copyrights are acknowledged and permission was sought, and granted, to reproduce the pictures shown in this work.

The front cover by Baxter-Cox Design.

ACKNOWLEDGMENTS

I would like to thank my good lady Sylvia for patience and perseverance. (These are her virtues and not her children.)

Jo, who did a great job putting words onto paper; it was a long slog.

Pamela Daniels (Editor) for her judicious use of the red pen.

Brian Prescott (Jade Publishing Limited), a thoroughly good bloke.

The afternamed people who kindly agreed to let me put names to incidents or accounts:

Paul Blagborough (P.A.B.)
Hugh Winterbottom
Maurice Buckley
James Humphreys
The Reverend Howard Gray
Christine Tinsley
Gordon Howard
John Fidler
Anne Declerq
Betty Whitehead (Taylor) for supplying material
Phil Larder
Joan Smith
Joan Fullard

Mercy, for her help with editing.

With a thought for those no longer with us.

I'm sorry I couldn't contact Christopher Wrigley and I hope for his forbearance.

David J. Lavisher
August, 2002

FOREWORD

It is reasonable to assume that northern village life in the late 'forties to late 'fifties of the twentieth century has been well documented by many people. However, they didn't live in our village and being the type of person who won't duck a challenge, given even ground, I thought I might open a few cupboards (having gathered the keys) and hope the skeletons won't fall over themselves to get out.

The book isn't (nor ever was intended as) a reference guide to the village. What I have tried to portray is my view of the times and my part in them. The piece spans the period 1948–1955, and is set in the Pennine village of Moorside, two miles due east of Oldham and one mile short of the Yorkshire border. It was an outpost of the town (to keep Yorkshire folk at bay), accents were thicker than beef dripping butties and Miss Demeanour was discussed around everyone's dining table. Some of the effort is tongue in cheek (and anything else my cheek will allow) nonetheless it's typical for all that. If I seem indifferent to some goings-on it is because the unquestioning attitudes of those days demanded it.

David J. Lavisher
August, 2002

Higher Counthill

My village started at the top of Counthill Fowt. For anyone unfamiliar with the word "Fowt", it's dialect for Fold. The Fold comprised seven houses, Mills's farmhouse and a few farm outbuildings. One of the houses served as a tack room-cum-tool store. On autumn days the wind fairly whistled up the passageway between the pigsty and the small shippon, driving before it strands of hay, people's hats, the odd chicken, my grandma's washing, someone's false teeth, anything that wasn't nailed down.

Black thunderclouds gathered so low and heavy over Strinesdale's reservoirs that the bats came out for their evening meal.

Counthill at that time of year was a place where Custer would quite happily have made his last stand – on a hill, the outlook bleak and nowhere to go. On the plus side, happiness came in the shape of long, lark-singing days, warm air fluttering against your face like a butterfly's wings, relative peace and quiet with few parental outdoor restrictions.

Haymaking was loosely forked hay loaded straight onto the cart.

Sunny days it was courtesy of the Lord. On rainy days – well, everyone knows it's the Government's fault.

Our house had small bedroom windows. In the descending dusk the hillside towards Roebuck would be sprinkled with tiny glittering lights, everything was so still. I can remember counting how many stars I could fit, along with the moon, into a single window frame on warm, late summer nights. A large, yellow, harvest moon would take up four windows and a bit of bedroom wall as it rose above Winterbottom's top shippon. If I woke up in the dark there was always a lion crouched in the stairwell. Mainly due to one Edgar Rice Burroughs, I suppose. After dark, a dog howled non-stop over towards Roebuck Lows. It was pleasant company until I fell asleep. I would probably consider it a nuisance now and sue its owners out of their birthright. Well, I might speak gruffly to them about it.

Turn to the right at "top o t'fowt" and the unmade road was known as the "flats" (meaning levels) and was anything but. The surface had more craters than an egg tray.

Bike riding on the flats was a demanding, jaw-breaking experience, not good news either for anything foolish enough to be relaxing in your stomach.

There were and are five terraced houses, one partly extended forwards to make a sweet and ice cream shop for passing strollers. I expect it caught pupils from Counthill Grammar School later on. The shop is now history and the extension is someone's front room. Mr and Mrs Massey owned the shop. Mr Massey had that unnerving approach to sales that fairground men have so ably perfected. He would hold his hand out for your money, say "Wadaya want?" and then "we 'ave none", and be on his way back into the house leaving the customer slightly befuddled about the shop's real purpose. (Mrs Massey was more patient with her young customers and always had a nice greeting when you presented your nose and eyes above the counter before spending twenty minutes choosing a ha'penny Spanish and a penny lolly.) Mr Massey's parting shot as he retired through the curtained doorway was "Don't bang the door, I'm watching thi." If he had said, "Don't bang the door I've got a headache," or "Don't bang the door it's falling off," he would have gained a lot more sympathy from a practising door banger like myself. All kids have a door-banging gene anyway. According to my Uncle James, Mr Massey was a blacksmith's striker in the smithy at Moorside during the working week.

A few cottages around Winterbottom's farm made up the "flats" dwellings.

One of these gave shelter to some relatives of mine, the Crisham family. They had a daughter Ann, who married my Uncle James and they produced two offspring, my cousins Joe and Ann.

Turning left down Counthill Road brought two cottages, one bungalow and the Grammar School with a caretaker's house (built later) in the school grounds. The Grammar School was off the drawing board and at the footings-and-a-few-walls stage during the Second World War. Started before the war and abandoned in case Hitler didn't like it and flattened it again, it stayed that way until its completion in 1951. I was able to play in the half-built superstructure, but only if my parents didn't know. There would be cows wandering about inside and, on heart-thumping occasions, other people.

Winston Churchill was supposed to come and attend the opening of the school, and the Council in a flush of zealous inspiration, laid tarmac on the road up to 20 yards past the school boundary fence but no further. You might consider that Mr Churchill would be walking backwards and not see the other 200-yard stretch of bleached white, pot-holed, unmade surface. Anyway, there might have been trouble in Havana and his cigar supply had been cut off, or perhaps he decided that his painting hobby was the better option because he didn't turn up. It's more than likely however that he was Prime Minister at the time. Having a good row in the House of Commons is better than having a shouting match with a Force 10 gale at Counthill you might think.

Funny how lines cross in later years. My wife's cousin, one John Fidler, was pupil and teacher all of his scholastic life at the school. So he should be good for a plaque or bust, even if it's only for services to canteen dinners. He won't mind my frivolity, I hope. John has a good story about rice pudding and school dinners. John attended Counthill Grammar School as a pupil when the school first opened for business. Initially the pupils were segregated at dinnertime, boys sitting down together first and the girls following when the boys had finished eating. No sex discrimination there then! John, who liked his rice pudding either home-cooked or from a tin had an aversion to the rice pudding cooked on the school premises. One day when the school-cooked variety was on the menu John asked the youngster who was serving the sweet at his table not to bring him any – so he didn't. Miss Moorhouse, English teacher and duty supervisor for that day's nutrition intake, seeing John without any sweet, asked him why that was. John replied that he didn't like school rice pudding. Miss Moorhouse decided that John was having some, like it or not, and instructed that a plate be filled and placed in front of him. John, an affable character most of the time, put the shutters up and refused to eat it, sitting staring at the plate and its contents as if it was a bowl full of plague. Some twenty minutes passed with the rest of the lads slowly drifting away as they finished eating, leaving John and the plate full of cold rice pudding staring at each other. Girl pupils coming in to eat their dinner found him contemplating his rice pudding and still occuping a seat – and therefore a place – that should have been taken up by a girl. Miss Moorhouse had disappeared by this time and John – brassed off by now and in rebellious mood – decided that some form of action was called for. He picked up the plate full of rice pudding and set forth to go and see the headmaster about his problem. The headmaster answered John's knock on the door bidding

3

him enter. Mr Bradley looked suspiciously at the plate as John entered his study and then asked him what he intended doing with the rice pudding. Heartily fed up with the whole business, John offered Mr Bradley the rice pudding saying, "Would you like a rice pudding, Sir?" Mr Bradley looked at the rice pudding again and then at John before replying, "I most certainly would not, I dislike rice pudding". John said, "I don't like it either, so I'll return it to the kitchen". Nothing was ever said about the incident again.

Across the road lower down Counthill Road, opposite the present-day Saffron Drive, were an asbestos, chalet-type bungalow and next door, a dwelling hidden by a privet hedge and rambling roses. I'm almost certain it was a converted railway carriage, and then I think, how and why? and my mind shuffles off to safer territory. Safety for me ended there and "no man's land" started. This was Barrowshaw Estate, where repute would have coal kept in the bath and children eaten for tea. The mixture of exiled town's people, a lot of roaming, fighting dogs, tough kids and handy pubs forges this kind of reputation.

I can tell you that I was bowel-testingly scared of passing the place.

My father's ideas on child management could be likened to the distance between the Sun and Jupiter when compared to the politically-correct welfare folk of today. I admire the latter to some degree – but not all. Father thought the best way to cure a fear of lions was to throw you to them. My daily task at the ages of seven and eight was to go down Counthill Road to Catterall's newsagents at Watersheddings for the evening paper, winter and summer, light nights or not. Dark nights had a particularly bad side to them, the Barrowshaw kids couldn't be seen because they'd broken all the street lights and there is an innate fear of darkness in all kids. I well recall thinking that I could hear ticking sounds as I walked blindly into the gloom and when I stopped, so did the tick. I would have legged it but not having an inbuilt compass is a bit of a bind when you're young. The "Where's my blunderbuss?" thought was uppermost in my mind, when footsteps I thought were my own carried on when I had stopped walking. The eerie glow of a cigarette was quite welcoming oddly enough, but a disembodied cough would have me rooted, holding my breath until my ears popped and my nerves twanged like Granddad's braces. Blundering into an adult would remove years from both our life expectancies. It introduced me to swearing and dancing in the dark. I expect everyone has done the pavement two-step; well it's a bit like that, except that there is a strong probability that you'll both end up on the floor terrified. All this was because my Dad didn't like that Chapman bloke, at the newsagents in Moorside.

Misery was a place I visited often.

Character-building as the experience was, self-preservation comes above all else. It is firmly fixed in my make-up, and I've utilised it unstintingly whenever it's been called upon. And I can assure you it has.

The access most used to our home was Haven Lane. The lane meanders down to the village. In doing so it passes bungalows (not built in my childhood) numerous semi-detached and a few terraced houses. High-walled fields afforded some protection if Marshall's spaniel was on the loose; he didn't bite (he didn't get a chance) but he barked like an echo in a biscuit tin. American Indians couldn't tiptoe like I did. Marshalls lived in the top "semi", the other half of which was Larders', Philip of the rugby playing, England managing C.V. At the time he was no more likely to be playing rugby than I was going to become an astronaut. He did, I didn't. On the odd occasion I called for Phil on my way to school I found he had perfected a novel method of entering his gabardine raincoat. He placed the raincoat in front of him, lining outside, placed his arms in the sleeves and threw the body of the coat over his head. One swift movement – coat on. No matter how I tried to emulate the feat at home, the coat always ended in my face or wrapped round my neck. I had to revert to the endless, find the sleeve-hole routine. He had a similar attitude as a long-striding centre, slipping the ball to wing, with much the same dexterity. Moorside produced its share of rugby players: Phil Larder, Edgar Brooks, Fred Ashworth, Alan Ogden and Tommy Reese all were or became, big league players.

Back from Haven Lane and across from Alexandra Terrace were the remains of Haven House (more about this later) demolished before my time. Next came the Council-run nursery, which at this time of writing is a Youth and Community establishment. My sister attended the nursery and wasn't ecstatic about it. She had a consummate dislike of cod liver oil which was administered daily on a very large spoon. She would be two or three years old, and under no circumstances was the vile stuff passing her vocal chords. People came for miles to watch her perform, Jean could scowl for England when in confrontation mode, which was fairly often. You might think

ink stains are stubborn to move, you've no idea! After a lot of cajoling, offers of toffees and downright threatening she would accept the stuff beyond her lips. Her face would set and then it was just a matter of time before we saw the repulsive stuff. I'm told that initially she would wait until I and our mother had gone and then give it back with a satisfied burp all down the front of her frock. This action led to my mother waiting until she thought it had been swallowed – a sort of Mexican stand-off. Jean has or had the patience of a broken-fingered needle-threader and could wait all day. Mother had to go to work. What can I say? Jean developed an individual line in communication skills; she would nod or shake her head – that's all. Any need for speech from her must have been associated with mouth opening and in turn with cod liver oil. Jean and her family now live in South Australia. Her life-long friend Sally lives nearby. My sister and I have always got on well, partly because she was always good for a "borrow" when I was a skint teenager but mainly because she has "attitude". I like that in a person.

Parkfield Mill took up most of the lower left-hand side of the lane apart from a row of subterranean air raid shelters, all gone now and the land built upon. The end triangular section behind the butcher's, where the lane joined Ripponden Road, housed the shelters. So on quiet moonlit nights, if the roar of twin Daimler Benz engines attached to a Heinkel 111 bomber, suddenly rumbles through your bedroom, those of you living in those new dwellings now know why it's happening.

Opposite the mill on the right-hand side was the ashes tip belonging to the mills. A chap named Harry Dawson, who was a "carter", spent his working days moving ashes, with his horse and cart, from both of the mills and tipping them at the rear of the Parkfield Mill. Whenever I saw Harry, he seemed to be dressed in rags and covered in fine dust. The ashes tip was spread around the base of a wondrously-high mill chimney, complete with lightning conductor in the shape of a cross (which may have been significant) attached to a metal strip, that ran down to earth any lightning which struck the chimney. Should that event occur, any poor devil leaning near the strip would be crisply barbequed on both sides and served with cold potatoes and tossed salad with just a dash of Yorkshire relish.

After the mill lodge came a couple of very old cottages – a lad named Bernard Short lived in the one next to the lodge – some more terraced houses and the blacksmith's shop or smithy pronounced "the" rather than "th". I don't know when blacksmithing ceased there;

except that the smithy became Oldham Diesels and later a design business. The last time I passed the building it looked empty. The smithy for the most part smelled of horse muck and burning hoofs from when the red-hot, newly-forged shoe was introduced to the hoof in the fitting process. I can't remember the blacksmith's name, it was something like "Geroutovere".

The lane was home to eight gas lamps, excluding the two attached to the walls of the mill. At this point I will own up to being an infant vandal. For some reason my best pal and I were hooked on the sound of shattering glass. The danger of anyone seeing us must have been part of the attraction. Walking home in the dark bore testimony to this anti-social pastime. The fact that my backside was well paddled and my pal's was equally well acquainted with his father's belt didn't seem to stop us at all. We never considered that we were the only two lads of stone-throwing age at that time who lived at the top of the lane.

Much of my early childhood seemed to be concerned with ration books and "The War". This latter was referred to often and for all I knew could have been something growing on an allotment.

"How's the war going on?"

The reply might be, "Ah well you know how it is Mrs Timkins. horse manure isn't like it used to be, mi' sprouts are full of blackspot, mi' potatoes have nittlewort and mi' musuntcastaspersions 'ave gone all droopy, and that Hitler chap isn't helping much either."

To qualify as a Moorsider in the early part of the last century, you had to be born within shouting distance of Moorside Mill. (Well! It's a bit of a bellow from Counthill I can tell you.) I wonder what the requirement is these days? Just knowing someone I suppose. There was a time when I knew the names of all the occupants of every house, the name of their dog and what they ate for breakfast. That's how it was.

Me and Mine

One of my earliest recollections is of this stranger wandering about the house, someone I had never met before, who insisted on both of us donning large pairs of olive-coloured, ex-army boxing gloves so he could punch me on the nose. This arrangement was not compatible with my lifestyle up to then, which went along the lines of "hand the little love to me" or "isn't he lovely" and "don't cry, here's a triple Neapolitan ice-cream", these uttered by warm, smiling young women of my mother's age. I didn't complain about the sentiments then, and I haven't done since, the ice-cream bit notwithstanding. Nose punching was a pastime one of us didn't enjoy, so strategy was required. I cried. That didn't work; the strategy box was empty and life with my father began.

Father returned from the army or the war bringing a kit bag full of discipline, a Yorkshire Terrier named Freddie, and because he was a "townie", a lot of smart answers. I can only put his dislike of me down to the fact that I was *in situ* and therefore in pole position, so to speak.

That happy if imaginative state known as Eden, left our house and flitted to my Auntie Ann's, never to return.

Auntie Ann married Armande Declerq of the French muffin-making family, whose shop was on the corner of Brunswick Street, at the Star Inn end of Union Street, Oldham. Auntie Ann thought the sun shone out of me and provided a refuge when things got tough at home.

A side note to that was my Cousin Christine. She was blonde, beautiful and twelve months my junior. I thought she was wonderful and it would seem she did too. She took it upon herself to improve her hairdresser-trimmed fringe, thus making it "contemporary". Scissors and children, fringes and frayed ends! A local photographer was summoned to capture the results; the photo in sepia is knocking around somewhere in the family.

Anyway, my father was a product of Oldham's back streets. On the few occasions that he unburdened himself (unburdening in his opinion was something that men didn't do), he said that he had brought himself and his siblings to maturity because his father was a drinker. This would be so; on the few visits we paid to our grandparent's home, Granddad wasn't there, or if he was, he was mostly in bed. He gave me a few coppers when I did see him, therefore denying the landlord at The Prince of Wales, Spencer Street, his annual holiday in Bermuda. When Granddad was "topped up", I could polish his totally bald head. I much admired his falling-off-the-chair act, which he could do without warning. Drinking pubs dry seemed to be his aim, putting food on the table was probably dependent on the flip of a coin, the coin would be a double-headed penny and the table lost out.

The amount of beer lurching around the town in waistcoat-covered bellies at any given time would have half-filled Moorside Mill lodge, according to my Gran.

When my Dad had finished travelling the world (with stints of army leave, of course) for the seven-year duration, he came home, chucked his medals in a drawer, got his pipe out (always a cherrywood Dr Plumb) bought some slippers (he could easily wear holes in), a comfortable chair (reserved for himself) and proceeded to get his feet as far up the chimney as the heat would allow. A broadsheet newspaper completed his idea of heaven. He didn't drink alcohol of any kind until his later years.

Father was mechanically-minded, as his stint in the Royal Electrical and Mechanical Engineers would suggest. He was being mechanically-minded one time, by putting his motorbike in the hallway and allowing it to leak oil all over our mother's bright red carpet. Needless to say, mother blew a fuse and sent the whole neighbourhood scurrying for cover. Her comments were firmly scorched into the wallpaper. Actually, father joined the Royal Artillery with his mate but I suppose the constant banging kept him awake, so he went to night school in the army (sounds daft) sat some exams and quickly transferred to R.E.M.E.

Being so minded, upon leaving the army he purchased a motorbike and sidecar, the requisite half dozen items of thick clothing, a huge, black, rubberised trench-type overcoat, a nebbed hat with flaps that came down over his ears in winter, producing temporary deafness, and gauntlets like stumping gloves. When fully rigged he looked like a large aubergine wobbling around. The motorcycles he owned in his life were always 500 cc single cylinders of the high compression variety. When he kick-started them, they often kicked him back.

10

I'm sure I wasn't the only one who enjoyed watching him hop all over our Jean's abandoned hop-flag pitch whilst holding the offended shin and swearing in bad temper. Our father could screw his face up like a baby with a sucked lemon when he was of a mind to.

He swore a lot. Well, quite a lot anyway.

Going abroad for holidays wasn't on because he'd been "everywhere". We saw a lot of Ilfracombe and later Torquay. We saw a bit of the East Lancashire Road on sunny days. The motorcycle outfit was dragged out and we would arrive, park on the grass verge along with half of Lancashire, get the primus stove out and make tea. My sister and I would be invited to watch the traffic passing by and then we went home. Wasn't life grand! Kids today only get to spend a fiver at McDonald's, buy two computer games every Saturday and visit Disneyland every year, so they don't know what they're missing do they?

Motorcycle journeys to these places were arduous to say the least. Sidecar sickness meant I spent a lot of time on the pillion seat, which was fine except that pipe smokers spend a lot of their life spitting out. Anticipating this form of social discourtesy was something of a lottery. I clearly remember a chap on a solo motorcycle pulling alongside us, wiping his face and waving a fist in fury at my Dad. However, Dad looked quite big in his Oliver Hardy outfit.

We must have eaten en route and tea came with egg sandwiches which were things to be regurgitated a few miles down the road. The fact that I didn't like eggs, and never have, didn't seem to stop them finding their way onto my sandwiches. Jam and chips rated high on my choice of child foods. Chips were difficult to come by at 10.30 am, not so jam, and not so nowadays.

Radio listening was one of Dad's favourite pastimes, particularly Sunday nights before the advent of television. We listened to "Journey into Space", or as he was wont to observe "A trip through your mind" (how well he knew me!) and "Riders of the Range". We could also listen to the Ovalteenies and a bloke named Horace Bachelor who was selling a get-rich scheme. He would tell/sell you his secrets that would enable you to win the pools. It wouldn't have occurred to a lot of people that if the scheme was so good, why didn't he own the world, or at least England. After that, bed. Bed was at 7 pm summer and winter, there was no flexibility at all. On the occasions when I wasn't in by seven o'clock, which was every night, a rather odd game of kick-your-behind, punctuated with the words "what do I keep telling you?" took place (Come to think of it I was quite a good sprinter at school.) I learned early to be out of the blocks very quickly. However, I could only run home and hope my mother was in; even this didn't save me most of the time. Telling the time is an accomplishment that necessitates a timepiece or watch. I didn't have one. My father was fairly brutal when I broke his rules, and I can differentiate between brutal and strict. He was unapproachable when I was young and of course when I grew older I didn't want to know. That's how it was. The same circumstances must have prevailed up and down the country, but I tell you it took some getting through. I should be grateful for having had a roof over my head, and food on the table, some kids wouldn't have had even that, I expect.

My mother was a product of the village, living most of her young life with her grandmother at 572 Ripponden Road, Moorside. I think the family had a "flexible" arrangement with its child-rearing practices, primarily because the four-house block was family-owned. Two houses fronted the main road with two joined on at the rear, back-to-back houses. Various uncles and aunts of my mother occupied the premises.

More importantly, you might think, was that my mother's mother had a liking for The Highfield Inn public house. It's reasonable to think that in her husband's absence in the army, he being a regular soldier, a few draughts or drams would act as substitute on a regular basis. Cuddling up to a skinful of ale rather than a skinful of male could have distinct advantages. It doesn't need supper making, doesn't make rude noises during the night, and of course doesn't present itself for breakfast at noon the next day. Mother was one of four children and had some female friends in the village, Joan Short (now Fullard), Enid Lawton and later Florence Mills, at least until my Dad returned from the war, from then on, no siblings, no friends. Her schooling needs were met by St Thomas's Church School, Moorside, from infancy to her leaving at the age of fourteen.

A variety of shops provided children's requirements then, as they did in my time, clothing and bicycles were the exception.

The lack of television meant playing whatever games were in vogue in the mid/late 'twenties. These would be outside pursuits, by and large. Who was pursuing whom she hasn't said to date. Mother was and still is, word perfect on some pastimes, despite the debilitation of an unremitting brain illness. She was a woman of her time, and deserves a better hand than life is now dealing her.

She was driven throughout her working life by the work ethic and no one was going to get in her way, not Adolf Hitler, Harold Wilson, the sugar plum fairy and certainly not me. Nobody did. Ringing down the years was that very true sentiment, "if you want anything you've got to work for it". "Anything" duly arrived in regular amounts, large expensive polished-console televisions, wall-to-wall carpets, good clothes and holidays. Curiously, we had to earn our pocket money, which didn't fill any pockets I ever owned. No housework, no money, and no good. Sixpence a week was the going rate. Mother spent a lot of home time polishing stuff, wielding a Ewbank hand-driven carpet sweeper industriously, and dreaming of vacuum cleaners. I always thought she was trying to wear out the pile so that she could buy a new carpet. She spent some time hanging rugs on the washing line and beating the living daylights out of them. More dust came out of those rugs than ever went into them. The Lord alone knows where it came from! The egg-sized mounds of dust were achieved by the enthusiastic application of a long-handled cane with an ace-of-clubs headpiece about the size of a dinner plate, kept in my wardrobe, out of my father's way. (Its value as a backside paddle looked pretty obvious to me.) While carpet-beating activities were in progress the danger zone was about two yards square and each lusty thwack was accompanied by "uh!". A double-handed forehand volley to tennis *aficionados*.

Cake making was her *forté* while we were young, from scones right up to wedding-cake standard. Meaning that Sainsbury's didn't come knocking with dozens of help-you items, or Nigella wasn't waiting behind the television screen for some wonderful confection to go belly-up in your digitally-operated-no-hands-needed kitchen kiln. Ovens were of the fireside hob variety, mainly used for bread making with the upper outer shelf to keep slippers and the cat warm.

It's possible that because of my need to vacate the premises at every opportunity, I didn't see any other side to her than the "background" person she appeared to be. I suppose her whole lifestyle could have passed me by in my youth and I never knew anything about it. I doubt it though.

In my childhood, indicators of social status were usually based on the size of things, much like today only more so. Large babies meant healthy, large cars meant wealthy, large policemen meant stealthy, that sort of thing. We were roughly in the middle of the arrangement. This I know because we had middle-sized prams known as half-coach-built perambulators or HCBs. One of these Silver Cross vehicles in white took up residence under the back inside window. It had an occupant, and it certainly wasn't me. Needless to say, the punched nose was put further out of joint by the arrival of my sister, five years later. Much as I liked her, my life would have been considerably easier had she shown a bit-of-willingness to be born first. A brother who was born between the two of us didn't live long. He was thought to have been asphyxiated by his cot blankets. I suspect he fell victim to cot death syndrome although we didn't know that then. Now we know what to call it – but still don't know what causes it. I suppose that's progress of a sort. John occupies a small plot in the village churchyard, the same plot I hope to join him in someday. There's something so final about cremation.

My Uncle James (whom you will meet later) said that the snow at Counthill was so deep in Haven Lane on the day of John's funeral, that his small coffin had to be carried down the meadow flanking the top of the lane, which is six feet or so higher than the road surface. They left the meadow at the unmade road opposite Alexandra Terrace. The family headed by my father carrying the coffin had to flounder through drifts into the village as best they could. How did they find the new grave? Who dug it out, I wonder? Not a labour of love you might think.

Neighbours

We lived at 78 Higher Counthill, which is now 76 and incorporates the Bradsell house next door, taking that house number.

Jack and Kitty Bradsell kept greyhounds, running them at Watersheddings track and probably Belle Vue, Manchester. There was little room in their house for ornaments because it was full of trophies.

One of their charges, Blackie by name, was responsible for catching a troublesome fox over by Strinesdale reservoirs one moonlit night. My mother had a sepia photograph of the two contenders at rest. Well the fox was more at rest than Blackie was I suppose. When I was about six or seven years old they had a housedog named Flash who took it upon himself to bite someone. Large Alsatians don't know they aren't allowed to do this and the resultant furore filled many column inches of space in the *Oldham Evening Chronicle*. The article carried a photograph showing my toddler sister Jean and Flash, the bitee, in close proximity. The fact that he wasn't sprawled across her, chewing thoughtfully on her leg, must have indicated to anyone interested that he wasn't dangerous. Small comfort for the bitten one I suppose. Maybe the police or the *Chron* or even the dog, were having a quiet day. Who knows what makes news? I don't know what happened to the dog; perhaps he was just a flash in the pan. The Bradsells were nice people and good neighbours.

Our house was a one room up, one down, slop-stone sink, flag-floor cottage with pantry. Toilets were across the yard and they were shared, two pairs with an ashes pit between them. They were so far away I often forgot what I was going for, and if they were occupied, cross everything including your eyes and think of England! The whole microcosm fitted snugly in amongst the farm buildings. Who owned the one-room palaces I'm not sure but they didn't half pong on hot days, yet people would occupy them for ages. (The toilets were known as "petty-cans" and were emptied on a weekly basis by the "night-soil gang" or the "midnight mechanics" as they were also known.) If someone walked across the yard with a newspaper and a purposeful air, only a well-aimed bomb, or a shout of "your dinner's ready" would deflect them.

Old farms are now viewed differently than, say, five decades ago. One eye looks firmly at their conversion into large domestic dwellings, the other looks sideways at the Ministry of Agriculture, or the European Parliament; grants are available, and not the scotch whisky variety either. They are also viewed in the manner of the American idyll.

Long golden days and Johnnie Hayseed men, bronzed, forking hay onto wagons, drinking homemade cider and gazing into the sunset. In reality, farms were dangerous places for the unwary, chock full of open-blade mowing machines, horses without ABS brakes etc, razor-sharp scythes, all quite good at removing digits, even whole limbs, while giving the appearance of serenity and goodwill. Tractors hadn't appeared on the small farms at that time, so horses still had the floor, so to speak. They entertained themselves by kicking folk into Yorkshire whenever they felt frisky. Parts of the farm were a proving ground on which my mother and the manure placings fought a constant war over my skin and clothes.

I remember falling into the muck midden, without any kind of flourish or any attempt at dignity. Showing off is a characteristic of oafs, and something I'm fairly good at. So I attempted to push an empty muck barrow up the midden plank onto the top of the pile, in much the same style as the men did. A historical or hysterical fact is that wheelbarrows like to do their own thing and we swiftly parted company. A hosepipe used for swilling the shippons down, was brought into play and it applied water vigorously to my far-from-fragrant personage. I've always believed that the amount of manure I swallowed was a major contributor in my race to achieve a height of six feet no inches (slightly more in cowboy boots).

The inhabitants of the farm outbuildings were often prone to displays of petulance; one such creature was a farm's cockerel, a rooster in the pterodactyl mould. He was not overly enthusiastic about children wandering amongst his womenfolk, even less about the removal of his shell-covered offspring. A good rooster could rise to two feet six inches tall, a small child about the same – no contest then.

Mills's farm ran a dairy herd, Friesian cows mainly, with a couple of Jerseys and the odd Guernsey. They also had a Friesian bull whose ambition in life was to strive for excellence in various acts of

16

malevolence. He was kept in a secure pen in the proven hole (fodder store) and took his exercise, apart from his duties, by trying to remove from their moorings the inch-thick planks surrounding him. He paid little attention to the neck chain he was tethered by and vented his spleen on the metal feed bucket in the box with him, only when he had finished dining of course. When the mutilation had been completed to his satisfaction, he would weigh you up, in the manner of a tramp at a banquet observing food.

"Want some of that then?"

"Who me? Er! No thanks!"

There was a pigsty accommodating one boar and two sows. They just lay around making the place untidy and grunting occasionally. Squealing occurred at feeding time and presumably if the conversation turned to the abattoir on Mortar Street at Hillstores.

James Humphreys was my uncle; he found the title amusing because of our difference in years, which was not much. He had an infectious laugh, incisive wit, paid his beer round with some reluctance, nurtured a few sleepy brain cells and everybody liked him. A nicer bloke I've never met. He was the youngest of my mother's siblings, and as is usually the case, of little consequence in the overall scheme of things. He spent much of his working life at Her Majesty's Stationery Office on Broadway, Chadderton.

James left St Thomas's School, Moorside, with two job options, working in Brookes's bakery in Ripponden Road or on Winterbottom's farm. He chose the latter. In the eighteen months or so that he worked there he gained enough knowledge to get himself a job on a Devonshire farm. Bigger southern wages and perhaps a bit of "leaving this one-horse town" influenced his decision. Not exactly a move across the road in those days.

He confirms a story I'd been told by Billy Massey when I was a youngster.

Mr Winterbottom, or "Owd Hugh" as he was known, took out a milk float on Saturdays, presumably to collect the week's dues because people worked during the week. If memory serves me correctly such floats usually carried two large churns at the rear, partly to take some weight off the cart shafts because it was less heavy for the horse's back but mainly for ease of access. The churns would have either taps or pint/half-pint ladles with long handles, to plumb the depths as the milk level fell. There would be smaller churns of Jersey milk or some ready-filled bottles and stacks of eggs plus a raincoat.

17

There was a holster on the corner of the float for the long slender horsewhip, and this item was invariably flourished with some *elan*, very rarely used, just flourished. Perhaps the silhouette of whip to hand, looked well against the sunrise – these days mechanised milkmen flourish mobile phones. Obviously as the round progressed away from the farm the weight on the float became less. "Owd Hugh's" round ended in the vicinity of Cross Street, Bottom o' th' Moor, where on occasion he would enjoy the facilities of a betting club as they were known, mainly for the liquid lunch that it provided rather than anything else on offer. The horse used in pulling his milk float was named Jessie; she had the patience of a saint and the homing instincts of a racing pigeon. There would be times when "Owd Hugh" didn't get home at the usual hour, prompting the observation that "He'd done it again".

James, who worked seven days a week on the farm said that you could see Jessie and the cart coming along Counthill flats in the late afternoon but no visible sign of "Owd Hugh". Mr Winterbottom would be reclining on the cart floor in a fine condition with a smile on his face. Unhampered by the tribulations of everyday graft he might sometimes be asleep. He also stayed there until someone came to fetch him. If everyone was out, tough. I had an instinctive liking for the man although he only ever said "ow do young un!" The fact that he would speak to a child must have been enough.

Nine farms surrounded the village; homes to similar-sized small dairy herds, horses, poultry, pigs, ducks and a variety of working dogs. The breed of dog didn't seem to matter; the only requirement appeared to be a loud bark and the ability to kid you that it was asleep. I've been present at a few Oscar-winning performances of this type; the phrase "they shall not pass" must be written into a farm dog's contract.

Mills's farm and Winterbottom's were at Higher Counthill; Holroyd's Little End farm and Armitage's were both at Strinesdale. Jimmy Russell had Spout House farm, Greens had Sholver Moor farm, Hartley's was at Sholver Lane, Howard's at Sholver Green, and Frank Hough's at Hodge Clough. Asa Lees's and Besom Hill farm, King Lane, may not have been classed as Moorside.

It was grazing and hay-making land. Mills's had grown the swede vegetable behind Haven Lane and kale behind Highfield Terrace. I was not aware of anyone growing anything else, except maybe a little older. But I will be corrected on that I'm sure.

Farms are peculiar places if you look at them with a sympathetic eye. Old properties seem to have no recognisable symmetry with regard to their building or layout. It's as if someone has rolled them like dice. They have boundaries but no edges. Some buildings have lots of windows, others none. Almost all the doors and doorways are of different sizes. The buildings will be of different materials, and the roofs will vary from flat to conical, even domed. Invariably the approach roads were rough, yet softly trimmed, without visible lines. On sunny days, farms shimmer in the midday, late-summer heat, oases where nothing at all moves.

Even at a young age I could feel eyes watching me as I wandered in and out of the buildings, yet to all intents and purpose they were empty. Shafts of sunlight slanted through the windows, like white girders; there would be dust mites drifting in the light, looking for a dark corner to settle in. Blue "white-wash" on the walls in the shippons and stables was curled and cracked; any flakes that escaped lay along the floor like discarded crisps.

The sweet smell of hay in the mistal's rafters (the difference between a mistal and a shippon, in my understanding, is that a mistal has a wooden ceiling which acts as a floor upon which hay can be stored above the cattle, serving the dual purpose of keeping hay dry and the cattle underneath warm in winter) eddied around on any slight breeze that found its way in from the fields. As I have said, there was always the feeling of being watched, yet, save for cats and rats, the buildings were empty. On rainy days they were dark, dank and dour.

Around the perimeter fields, small unidentifiable buildings sat in crumbly isolation, like scraps tossed from a giant's table. Lying around the farmyard would be lumps of metal with no imaginable use, bits of leather with brass harness buckles, mouldering their way to obscurity, and stacks of old wood. On Sunday mornings, after milking, everyone got the rest of the day off, until evening milking anyway. "Wow!" According to Section 3 of the Farm Animals and Feathered Brethren Union Rulebook, cows might meet by the yard gate organising trips out, pigs can grunt and cavort hamming it up, and horses contemplate a day at the races, chickens can enjoy a rock concert in the long, dimly-lit, hen houses and ducks may waddle off orienteering or cruising on the big pond. I, with my fertile imagination, would eventually wake up in the barn or buttercup-filled sunny meadow, back from my roamings through the stratosphere seeking the whisperings of paradise, or wherever dreamers go when they lay their heads down.

19

Contrary to popular opinion, farms smell sweet most of the time, it is only when it rains that Kendal's parfumerie department is a better place to be.

Anyway, what can smell sweeter than a field of newly-mown hay, drying in the sun?

St Thomas's Church, Moorside

"A MOMENT"

Still, though the dawn has broken
The sun lies quiet on shivering stone.
From serried tombs no word is spoken.
Tired, the clocks march po-faced on.
Remote, the noisy world flies by
Beyond the green in another vale.
A whispered dream in the borders sigh,
(Some passing satyr chased his tail).
Slight feelings that I stand accused
From silent names stepping along.
Such rushing warmth of kin, imbues
A fleeting glimpse of youth's old song.
Blessings sought in the dreadful hour
Refuge, large, on a minute stage.
Your bosom draws the weakest flower
Leasing tenure from another age.
Across the fields and quibbling streams
This towering steepled spire rejoiced.
To sleepless and the frightful dream
The careless hour gives strident voice.
Good to look and feel your strength
Enjoy the rich, the stained-glass prize.
The door half-open down your length,
Half-closed to heedless passers-by.
This corner-stone of weighty span
In reverence laid by man for God.
Maybe God laid the stone for man
Among this coarse and pithy sod.

And I,
Yes I could lay at last to sleep
'Neath scudding skies and soaring lark
Among the patrons of the village, deep.

From a distant field a small dog barks.

Church and Chapel

I think that most of the village was churchgoing in my childhood. There were various denominations, namely Church of England, Chapel, and much later the Roman Catholic faith in what was the grounds of Moorside House. The Rev John Calderley captained our ship and was really well liked, although he could be a little pompous. I found his sermons terminally boring as a child. They had to run a specific length of time from the off and a lot of watch-watching went on among his congregation. He was definitely doze and fidget material.

He didn't harangue but his tone was stentorian, he was a great "into the distance" gazer and his singing voice was both bass and loud; microphones were unnecessary. Not that they were available at the time, they seemed to arrive with rock and roll vicars and he wasn't that either. Churches of all denominations "work"; people whisper their devotions in peace and quiet, seek solace, and are emotionally motivated by them. A devout person would go a long way to find a more comfortable and uninhibiting place to worship than St Thomas's, Moorside.

I liked the place as a child and nothing has changed materially or otherwise. If the Mellodew family (Mill owners and the village's principal employer) were looking for a monument to their generosity, they did themselves proud and many people have had the benefit.

It's a place I visit periodically not to worship but to wonder. I tidy the family grave occasionally while wondering. Quite a few of my ancestors are enjoying the facilities of the "B" graveyard and rejoice under the name of Wadsworth. Later family members are in the "C" section and have had their gravestones removed. I think opportunists removed a few rows of marble headstones some years ago when Sholver was in its preyday.

My mother judged the status of each deceased person by his or her location in the graveyard. "A", was the ground overlooking Northgate Lane and Grafton Street, accommodating the affluent and the most respected. The best seats were always at the front and the deceased would have first sightings of weddings, christenings and people about to be interred. "B", fronting Glebe Lane and the vicarage, was obviously less recognised but the occupants got the photo-shoots at weddings and listened in to the gossip. They also had the benefit of the sundial if the church clock needed winding. "C", running parallel to Sholver Lane, had to content itself with the daily passage of the vicar and the occasional glimpse of children in the schoolyard. "C" now has the Garden of Remembrance and is a resting place for a person of oriental extraction who is facing the opposite way to everyone else, maybe because of some religious requirement. My grandmother and brother are in "C" and within speaking distance of each other should the need ever "arise". It's quite likely our lot will have formed some kind of midnight focus group rather than while the time away doing nowt; getting into the modern-day spirit of things, so to speak. It would never have occurred to my mother that the grave placings were probably done on a continuity basis until each section was full. You wouldn't like to pass on and be buried next to someone you didn't get on with. Eternity is a long time.

The Rev Calderley left for pastures new, when or why, I've never known.

I have some knowledge of David Lawrence a later vicar. He seemed to me to be a clean man, which sounds odd. He was resplendent in crisp, bright whites when leading the congregation, had white teeth, fine spectacles and smiled as if he knew something I didn't. Maybe he did.

He wrote a comprehensive appraisal of the village's history during his tenure, named *The Parish Church of St Thomas, 1872–1972*. I was fortunate to be loaned a copy by Howard Gray, the present vicar. The book is fascinating reading. In our early years we think that nothing ever happened anywhere before we were born. Reading about history, particularly if it's pertinent to you and yours, changes that thinking. A feeling of belonging to the village (however short that period of time was) is how I felt after reading the book.

Howard, the man charged with the village's spiritual welfare for the last twenty-five years, is a person we could all aspire to be; no fuss, no frills and straight as you like.

Howard officiated at my wedding to the present Mrs Lavisher, and at the christening of one of her grandsons; everyone was comfortable.

He was a member of the committee responsible for the conversion of my old school into its present usage as a Church Hall. Often such buildings are demolished to make way for some modern glass and hardboard creations. If the building could speak it could tell us a darn sight more about Moorside than I know, and could divulge more about me than I'm prepared to tell.

When I visited the Church after a long absence, my first observation was that the sundial and column with stepped plinth were missing from outside the main doors. It appears that someone stole the sundial; the column and its plinth are now in the Garden of Remembrance. No doubt someone's garden will have gained in social standing from acquiring the piece, and all for a few quids' worth of beer money or whatever.

Generations of children have stood and tried to work out the time in summer and been told how it worked. I conjure up a picture of a still-life painting, showing Bob Berry's butcher's block, his meat cleaver, and the thief's fingers, whenever I think about the theft. Still, as Henry the Eighth probably said about his wives, "Once they've gone, they've gone for good".

The Glebe fields as we knew them, played host to games after the Whit walks. All the old familiar games took place, sack races, egg and spoon. Someone brought a donkey one year and gave rides, the whole thing was generally well organised.

To the right of the field ran Sholver Lane, some six feet below the standing ground. To the left, looking towards Heyside, ran a full row of pens or allotments, all enclosed by high wooden fencing. I never knew what they contained, except that one pen grunted occasionally and another had an excitable dog. Perhaps the dog was guarding prize-winning cabbages. The vicarage stood in its own grounds at the clock-tower end of the Church and had its own containing walls. The wall adjoining Glebe fields has kept a little-known fact to itself for many years. My Uncle James said that one of Mellodew's horses expired in the field and without further ado a few chaps ran out from the factory with shovels and an employee's worth of enthusiasm, dug a deep hole in the field next to the vicarage wall and interred the unfortunate animal. Whether excerpts from the funeral service were spoken over the site is a matter for conjecture. I'm not sure where in relation to the present dwellings the burial site is located, but make no bones about it, it would be a grave matter at the time. Neither the knacker's man nor the glue factory got their hands on that beastie.

Anyway who would want to provide the glue in a table and chairs set, eavesdropping on the lunchtime deliberations of a family pulling their neighbours to pieces and shredding the reputations of pillars of the community? There is no need to put the question to a vote, it can safely be said that the "Ayes" would win.

The graveyards surrounding the Church were not unpleasant places to while away time during the day. Nights, especially in winter, were a different story. Little or no light came from the gas lamps dotted about the place. We used to keep our nerves tuned up by venturing down Glebe Lane in small groups ready to leg it when the tension became too much. "Too much" was when a clap, clap, clap sound could be heard. The dead horse? Ghosts maybe? The flagpole lanyard more than likely. In the race to get away, falling was not an option. I've often wondered how fast top sprinters could go if they were really scared.

The village supported a Chapel, with the Methodists having a more relaxed attitude to things as far as I was concerned. I'm not sure if fire and brimstone raged within its walls. I'm sure it did occasionally, for somewhere in the fog of forgetfulness, a thought is running around about a visiting preacher who had a bag full of fire and brimstone and was going to chuck it all over everyone.

The lighter side of the Chapel's doings included the Christmas pantomimes, one of which was *Cinderella*. Such pastimes owed much to the diverse talents of the Chapel people themselves.

It dawned upon me early that we weren't all of the same religious persuasion when featured players I had never seen at our Church included newsagent John Chapman playing the part of one ugly sister and Mr Simpson, landlord at The Highfield Inn, looking just as ugly, playing the other. Barbara Simpson (not directly related to the publican) who lived next door to us, played principal boy in one production (I can't recall its name) and was high on my list of older girls to be awestruck by.

Mother Goose, another production, starred an older boy playing the goose from inside a *papier-mâché* creation. At times he couldn't speak his lines for laughing and tripped up frequently. The only bits of him visible were his legs, hanging down like two bell ropes. When he wandered towards the edge of the stage the front row of the audience lifted their arms to catch him, a bit like a Mexican wave. Much giggling accompanied these "staged" feints from the goose and quite a bit of "Woooing!" came from the rear seats as the front row involuntarily reached out to catch him and then sat on their hands in embarrassment as he wandered away from the edge. At times a piece of scenery got fed up with the proceedings and keeled over, scattering the players like a bucket full of frogs on a hot stone flag. A flustered individual would reposition it; then everyone had to wait while the dust settled. Usually, the resultant bouts of laughing, hiccoughing, and wet eye wiping had finished by the time we went home. Usually!

My mother, brought up strict Church, was apt to kick over the traces now and again, and patronise the Chapel plays. Anyone who commented upon our crossing the religious divide would have been told to mind their own business and anyway her ticket money was as good as anyone else's. When she was a young woman, the words "I'm wrong" weren't in her vocabulary. Character assassination runs deep within me!

A second merit mark went the Chapel's way at Whitsuntide or "walking round" as it was ungraciously known. The Chapel had engaged Black Dyke Mills Band on one occasion, which must have been a huge *coup* because of the awed whispering and exclamations at the beautifully-turned-out tunesmiths. They made us Church kids welcome at dinnertime on these occasions. After we had eaten dinner in our school hall with the Church, Bill (my pal) and I raced along behind Moorside Mill, jumped the brook and ran into the Chapel where we were given cake and biscuits.

No one played heck or whinged about it, at least, not within my hearing. I'm tuned into other people's consternation, I always have been. Cakes and kids rub along well. It was great!

During the Whitsuntide procession however, all was not necessarily great. The two sects, if by chance they should meet, stared straight ahead. According to my mother, on the following Monday, at work, everyone would carry on as if nothing unusual had happened. Such differences never bothered us kids. If our paths crossed, we used to talk across to the other denomination from between the lengths of rope used to keep us in line. I can't believe the ropes were to stop us escaping. I understand that a thawing-out took place later and that both groups walked together on occasion. At that time none of us had heard of Ecumenicism and I for one would have been unable to pronounce it anyway.

The Mill

It had gone.
Nothing, except weeds and rubble,
Although like the Pennines,
it had always been there;
The siren, opening and ending the day.
Powerful, black, grinding machinery
dwindling,
to humming, pirouetting lengths of gossamer.
Silver against the morning windows,
smelling of warm oil and cotton essence;
Tended by shadows
laughing and talking in signs
in the grey, lint-clouded haze.
The cold darkness of winter
lit by the night-soft, warm-glowing windows,
inviting on the lonely way home.
It presided over the village
like an ancient brooding sphinx
emitting silent rhythms along the winds
over the barren hills of the northland.
A way of life.

The Mills

When I was a child the name "Mellodew" was a constant. It ran around the dinner table, spending an enormous amount of time under my grandma's roof and entered conversations that had nothing to do with the family.

Everything seemed to be "at Mellodews". The family practically owned the village, its two mills (Moorside Mill on Northgate Lane and Parkfield Mill on Haven Lane), church and school. Benefactors and employers to the community, they built and owned most of the housing stock – long rows of terraced houses and other buildings, dotted about the place like scattered Smarties from a dropped box. They had the use of large black cars and dressed for Sunday every day. Their family homes were three large, detached properties in their own grounds. These were Haven House, in Haven Lane, which was demolished before my time. Holroyds, the farming family, lived in and ran a riding stable from the outbuildings within the grounds; Haslems lived in the adjoining cottage. The grounds were full to bursting with rhododendron bushes and other trees good for climbing. Holly bushes grew in the grounds, so did a rather unsociable dog. We could play Cowboys and Indians there. If the gates were shut and the dog prowling outside, we went home, our bottoms feeling more comfortable, still intact and sitting on chairs.

Parkfield House, on Ripponden Road was a quiet house, largish but always appearing to be unoccupied. It wasn't, it gave shelter to a bull mastiff! The property had a long, narrow, circular driveway, which eliminated the need for reversing the coaches or ponies and trap, which without firm guidance might knock things over and trample all over the flowerbeds. A high wall and many mature trees and shrubs bounded the grounds. Barry Simpson, The Highfield Inn's only son and I enjoyed hide and seek in there under the same conditions as in Haven House. The mastiff feigned indifference when we scaled the walls but we knew he wasn't slavering because of poor table manners; he had a full complement of well-ground teeth and wasn't employed to guard flowers. Discretion was required. Parkfield House Hotel and Country Club fills the whole of the grounds these days. The old house will be cowering under there somewhere, wondering what the heck it did to merit its present mode of employment: wedding receptions and other popular functions decidedly less genteel than the purpose it was built for. My wife and I held our wedding reception there. I looked for some acknowledgement from the house because of our shared experiences all those years ago. But the house just ignored me, staring stonily across Beal Valley as if I were to blame for its present circumstances.

The main Mellodew family dwelling was Moorside House opposite the Post Office, next to "Old Moorside" a little hamlet still there, where the family business in Moorside first began. The family had business interests elsewhere previously. Moorside House also was policed, this time by a pair of Afghan hounds or Borzois, possibly Salukis, anyway tall, hairy, spindly, things with knock-knees and no manners. Their favourite pastime involved waiting until a goodly amount of schoolchildren had gathered in front of the large, cast-iron gates, waiting to cross Ripponden Road under the supervision of a volunteer villager, then sticking their scrawny necks through a head-sized hole in the gate (the hole is still there unrepentant for its part in these episodes – can you have a fifty-year-old hole?) letting rip with a series of sharp, growly, foreign barks, thereby removing a lengthy amount of time from everyone's lifespan.

Plans to climb trees in that garden never got on the drawing board never mind off it!

Household and business stables were linked to the main house through a cobbled yard; there were cart sheds and a large tack room. The yard entrance was on Turf Pit Lane. Most of the buildings are still there at this time of writing but appear dishevelled now. I was assailed by a feeling of melancholy the last time I saw the place. I recall one of the coach houses giving shelter to a beautiful – stunningly beautiful -- lacquered chaise. I never saw it in use nor a horse of the type that would pull it. I remember yellow-spoked wheels and button leather upholstery; the shafts were kept in an upright position and also yellow. The inside smelled much like the 10,000 Italian, leather-handbag shops I've journeyed through with my wife. The whole place was alive then, with half-muffled thumps from a large, iron-shod hoof inside the buildings. Redolent with the heavy, warm smell of horse manure, wisps of straw gently lifting into the breeze, and flies; in the rain, the cobbles glittered. In hot summers the tar which separated each cobble would soften and with a little dexterity could be lifted and rolled into tar balls. Often the balls would go into your pocket to soften even further and there they remained. Washday was a day better spent elsewhere! Making up the perimeter wall and next to the gateway, a pair of semi-detached cottages fronted Turf Pit Lane. Tommy Cheetham and his spouse occupied the bottom one. Tommy drove the horse and cart that ferried cotton laps from Moorside Mill to Parkfield Mill. The cottages would be mill houses and for the workers, I presume.

Tommy, a tall, saturnine man with a large Adam's apple and tobacco-stained teeth, was given to distance gazing. He could often be seen leaning on the front door jamb, holding the house up, while smoking a cigarette. I can't recall him saying anything more than "Ow do" to anybody. He wore braces to keep his leather-belted trousers up (talk about insecurity), a check shirt and soft, "Sunday type" boots. The occupants of the other house won't reveal themselves to my memory, I have a feeling they were members of the Sunter family but I could be wrong about that. Nathan Sunter drove the Karrier Bantam truck for Mellodews. It was of the flatbed type with a canvas canopy and a small cab.

I liked Nathan; he was a largish man who wore collar and tie with bib-and-brace overalls. His most endearing asset however, was that he liked me.

This meant I could ride with him, whenever he wished.

I should explain. These acts of ecstasy took place during the four-week summer holiday from school (six weeks now). With a little imagination, the truck became a Spitfire, which was piloted from the passenger seat in the cab. "Passenger seat" is perhaps a grandiose title to give to the fixed toolbox draped with several old hessian sacks upon which I perched. At that time, a seat belt was administered by my father and was unrelated in any way to the article that now carries the name. Bill Haley didn't invent Rock and Roll, it was invented by Karrier Bantam. The sheet of aluminium that served as the vehicle's dashboard held a number of various-sized dials, to which Nathan seemed indifferent. He occasionally gave one a finger tap but that could have been affection rather than a need to ascertain anything.

Fuel gauges in those days were situated on the fuel tank itself. They were prone to great exaggeration and similarly, to damage. Nathan spent a great deal of time dipping the tank, usually with a wooden stick which, being absorbent, told lies about the tank's contents, or lack of them. The road to the fuel stillage was paved with dark mutterings, especially if the truck ran out of fuel betwixt the two mills.

Mellodew Street was a short, narrow street, not one you would associate readily with the Mellodew family. I have dim memories of its outside toilets with ash pits. The tiny terraced houses had little, natural stone, flag fronts, and small, wooden, felt-covered sheds were attached to the houses. The street was unmade and of a good cart-width, its surface covered, in parts, with house-fire ashes, in an attempt to level the deep-riven fissures that appeared in winter or after heavy rain. The houses were back-to-back with those on Sholver Lane. The street itself now seems to be incorporated into the properties, as gardens. Washing lines, criss-crossed from houses to toilets, were good for swinging on, and presumably a nuisance if the householders didn't remove them on dustbin day before running off to work.

A large part of my time during summer holidays was spent sitting on a big, green, wooden box at the end of a passageway in the Glebe Lane-end of Moorside Mill. Reading comics, twiddling my thumbs and wrestling with eight-year-old's problems, like the origin of the species, advanced mathematics, writing the Queen's speech, another war and its likely impact upon a chronically-bored child. In between I would wonder what was for dinner. Alternatively, I could spend time with Albert Mellor, the stoker, who looked after the three Lancashire boilers on the day shift in the "fire hole". He always had a spare sandwich, and muscles in his spit.

When the Mellodews built the mill, they also very thoughtfully built me a mill lodge (a large quantity of water contained nearby, used to create steam to provide power for the driveshafts in the mill) and I felt obliged to try and fill it in with stones. I tried fairly hard over a number of years but it just swallowed them up and resumed steaming gently.

It is worth mentioning in passing, that mill lodges were responsible for the creation of a number of seaworthy rafts of some ingenuity, constructed from barrels and laths tied with string, old cast-off doors with box seats, and cone skips tied together with washing line. An equal number of different examples will probably have followed the *Titanic* route, I suppose. Monday mornings would find these ill-assorted craft bobbing around in the oily, green water, looking ... well, wrecked. On the face of it, where better to earn your "Master Sailor's Ticket" than a warm-water mill lodge, in an oasis of green fields and stone walls.

To my knowledge no one drowned, although there would have been some fraught moments, I don't doubt.

Another form of regular entertainment was to cross the road to Parkfield Mill and irritate my grandmother into coughing up a few pennies.

These found their way either to Taylor's confectioners (they had pink meringue halves stuck together with stiff cream) or to Yates's confectioners next-door-but-one down. Their top position in my high-scoring points system was unassailable. They made the largest, flakiest, cream-filled, down-yer-jersey-front, vanilla slices on the planet. Come Friday, they sold small, round, corrugated cartons of sherry trifle with individual wooden spoons stuck into the cream. The spoons did it for me every time. The front of my jersey was still tolerably lick-able a good hour later.

One of my classmates at school, Brian Butterworth, had a relative who worked at the shop. A bit of tactical manoeuvring if there was a queue, would ensure my being served by her. I was convinced she gave me the biggest slices available and perhaps she did. If the shop was empty I could lean over the shop display partition and choose my own piece. The shop was particularly well lit and spacious, the space being full of warm aromas. The freshly-baked bread would come bustling in on a large wooden tray, usually carried by a turbaned lady with flour halfway up her arms. Large warm pies for the mill workers and golden sausage rolls glistening on the warm shelf, newly-baked shortbreads and multi-coloured iced cakes, decorated in ways only to be seen in France or Italy these days. Long rows of bread tins covered in linen or muslin waiting for the dough to rise; the yeast smell was tangible, it was so strong. I was recently reminded of this when we purchased bread from a superstore where we shop. The loaf was expensive, film-wrapped, packed with everything nutritious, more kinds of grain than spots on a leopard, and hadn't been touched by anything human. It was so sterile it didn't want to leave its wrapping and smelled of reconstituted cardboard after a night of being slept on by a travelling person.

A little hysteria is good now and again!

Small balls of cotton hung around the many exits from the two large mills in our village. It was as if they wanted to escape but hadn't the nerve to roll into the winds that blew up from Heyside. Drifts, formed in corners, clung tenaciously to weeds and rough stone walls.

Occasional flurries leapt half-heartedly into the air in little whorls, quickly subsiding, not wanting to attract anyone with a brush.

During the week, the village hummed – to use the more usual meaning of the word. Huge extractors roared out onto the surrounding roads, propeller blades spinning faster than the eye could follow. Always, thin streamers of dirty cotton jigged and whipped from the grimy cowling, until they broke free, eddying into stiffish breezes, which pushed them purposefully in the general direction of Yorkshire.

Machinery ground and clanked its way through the day, working towards the sound of the old air-raid siren moaning into life in late afternoon, signalling everyone to "go wom".

All day long, lights burned in the factories, regardless of bright sunshine, fog or anything else.

Without exception, the lower rows of windows on the ground floor levels were almost opaque. Pressing your eyes up to the dimpled glass would usually reveal the distorted figure of someone known to you. That was it, you just knew them. You may never have spoken, the workers could live miles away from the village and rarely be encountered once they had left the mills, but you knew them.

The whole mill experience was of a warm greyish gloom, wrapped in a hot oil smell. Realistically this wouldn't have been so. It is likely that the mills – with so many people working together – even in those days, were a hot-bed of scandal and intrigue. When the mills stopped work for the day the village was deathly quiet. You could hear the Church clock ticking.

The mill manager apart, I understand that the main chap in charge of the mechanical gubbins was the engineer or whatever grand title he worked under. As in most areas of life, the man who works the engine calls the tune. It goes without saying that the engine room was off-limits and very efficiently protected by a red and white sign saying "Keep Out". A small catch-you-asleep window was in the upper half of the door and accessible by chair.

The room held acres of polished brass rails and gleaming copper pipes, numerous clocks with black, flickering fingers, various gauges and steam valves, black cast-iron catwalks, cogs of different sizes, and great, many-toothed gear wheels attached to a body-thick drive shaft that vanished through a wall. Dangling from the very high ceiling was a series of lights. All the shades were green-backed metal, with white reflectors giving off a dull, warm glow. Although it was a veritable powerhouse, there was no movement.

Sitting in one corner, like an afterthought, were a small table and chair and the regulation locker. The table usually had on it a white billy-can and butty box; sometimes it held a man in blue overalls. If he was in attendance, a loud shout of "Oiy!" when he spotted me, resulted in my hastily dismounting from my chair, to safety, which oddly, was through the nearest door. I never felt the need to run any further. Large parts of the mill were accessible to me with permission, but more often than not without.

The place was a wonderland of black, clanking machinery and overhead pulleys. Leather belts six-inches wide or more, running from the ceiling-mounted drive-shaft pulleys to the machinery drive-wheels at ground level. The fast-rotating belts had a nasty habit of picking up unwary jacket-wearers and beating them against the ceiling. Spindles spun faster than the eye could see, and spinning frames running on tracks backwards and forwards remorselessly removed careless toes. Many of the workers didn't wear footwear of any kind while tying up the broken ends as they roved with the machines. Nobody had ever heard of steel toe-capped protective footwear. You know the type, they will protect you from a ten tonne load dropped from a height of five hundred feet, but you can't lift them to walk in. The factories were home to countless mutilating machines of one kind or another. They would render today's omnipotent Health and Safety officers apoplectic, and have your caring sharing counsellors leading you to the couch in their best hand-wringing manner should anything befall you. You will probably be advised to take three months' paid sickness leave and be able to sue someone for exposing you to the realities of life. In those days, it would be some compensation, a guaranteed job for life, and one shoe to accommodate four toes instead of five.

The essence of the mill for me was the hot, oily cotton smell of the place; people shouting a lot, and winter warmth. All the inside walls were painted, bottom half green, top half cream, with an inch-wide black belt to keep the cream half up. The canteen would be noise free when empty and seat one hundred or so at a time. All the rooms had rounded support columns a foot thick that ran into the distance in equally-spaced lines. Oiled wooden floor-boarding was fought over when being replaced because of its weatherproof qualities. Women with names like Nellie, Tilly, Jessie and Flo', all wore wrap-around flowered smocks, sometimes pinnies as well and turbans, and many wore clogs. The yelling of "Coo-ee" was meant to attract attention.

Because of the general noise everyone turned round like a roomful of oscillating fans on full speed to see if the caller wanted them.

Workers had odd titles like "little piecers", the licentiously-named "strippers and grinders", "mule tenters" and "card tenters".

It's possible if they went camping they would be canvas tenters!

Grey and lint-covered people drifted in and out of the rooms. There were many cotton "ghosts" with unremarkable, perhaps unnecessary, jobs but they were all pieces of the jigsaw that transforms the raw cotton into the velveteen woven as a final product.

A classmate had a granddad living in Turf Pit Lane who was a – or the – mill manager, named Mr Dawson. Mr Dawson was a character I recall with some affection, not least because he was short, portly and unhurried. We often met at the bottom of Turf Pit Lane because he went to work when I went to school. Black, pin-striped suits and bowler hat were his thing, a fob watch and chain adorned his amply-proportioned "weskit" and he wore mirror-gloss shoes. He never failed to say "Good morning", looking at the ground or admiring his polished shoes as he walked past me. He would have made a good model for a porcelain figurine. I say this without malice for he was a sharp image in an otherwise drab scene.

In order to "kill the mill" – using today's cretin speak – I should describe the mill engine's exhaust system game. Steam was vented in a rhythmic, "thumpah, thumpah", constantly-recurring fashion, as the exhaust valve opened and closed. The steam passing through a system of pipes which culminated in a cast-iron grid, some two feet square. The grid lifted and lowered in tandem with the valve vent, although no more than a few inches. All this took place in Northgate Lane, halfway along the side of the mill. You could place your school cap on the grid and watch it leap into the air from the exhaust. You could place yourself on the grid and leap into the air too. You could leap into the air again from the swift clout administered by a mill person who ran through a side door in agitated fashion. I presume that too much weight on the grid would have caused a build up of pressure likely to deposit us all on the nearest planet when implosion took place.

School

My introduction to St Thomas's Infant and Junior School at Moorside passed without fanfare or anguish so far as I remember. The school, situated at the Sholver end of Northgate Lane sat happily within the Church grounds and I'm told it was built before the Church.

When a child was introduced to the school for the first time it was met by Mrs Aubrook, a large lady with an imposing frontage, most of which was her lap. It was a comforting place for tearful four and five year-olds. Mrs Aubrook was an infant teacher. After their first year at school, the pupils of infant classes two and three had to be present because the three classes were quite small and close together. Because there is safety in numbers, the other infant teachers also attended induction. Two classes were held in the same room while the other class was taught in an adjoining room through a connecting door.

I recently reflected that small children run away from their mother at every opportunity, until the first day at school. The opposite occurs at this time and some children develop very long arms in their efforts not to be given over to the unknown.

Along with Paul Anthony Blagborough (who shall hereinafter be referred to as PAB), I was a St Ambrose, Watersheddings, nursery school squab. We did our novice class over twelve months, therefore when introduced to the infant school proper it was a piece of cake. Time spent in infant classes seemed to be taken up by papier-mâché model making, learning the times tables by rote, making strings of paper decorations for Christmas, and singing songs such as "Jesus wants me for a sunbeam". A bit odd really when we'd only recently arrived on the planet. Sunbeams in infant class three, came through the south windows, and were laden with dust specks and sleep-inducing heat.

Playing with Plasticine was generally accepted as being the best entertainment on offer. The stuff was good for the plugging up of water taps and door locks, it found its way under your nails and had a gritty texture if chewed. It was also useful for making multi-coloured cows and dogs to please the teacher. There was usually heck to play if it happened to get onto the wooden floor and trodden into the grooves between the boards, which it couldn't help but do because it was good for rolling into a small ball and throwing at someone.

I know for a fact that a largish ball of the stuff rested for some time on the reading-book cupboard gathering dust. If at the end of each lesson, a smaller volume was handed back to the collection monitor than was handed out, pockets had to be emptied, and corners searched. We were admonished regularly but nobody seemed to care much.

The school had seen both my mother and my grandmother pass through its portals and complete their education up to the age of fourteen. My generation was shipped out after the "eleven plus" exams, to wherever their scholastic bent could best be catered for. In my case it was to the Blue Coat School or Henshaw's Secondary Modern as it was known at the time, but that's another story.

St Thomas's had two playgrounds, a large one for the boys, and a narrow, flagged, corridor-like and at times sunless one, for the girls, adjacent to Sholver Lane. A five-foot-high separating wall next to the narrow entrance to the girls' yard stopped a lot of fanciful name-calling with the resultant plait-pulling when the boys lost their temper.

Entry to the school was through three doors, one of which was permanently locked (cutting down the escape routes). In the main school yard the large aperture admitted nine o'clock entry. Lines were formed in school year order, rain or shine and everyone filed inside supervised by the teacher on duty. This never prevented much giggling, pinching, rib poking and tongue displaying going on. At least, when Mr Wrigley (Pop Wrigley to us lads), was overseeing proceedings. He was a large man (or he appeared so to me) with a very short fuse, drove a Morris Minor from Delph to school each day, except when the car objected and was accomplished in the art of chalk and blackboard duster throwing. He must have had psychic tendencies because he always knew who was whispering whenever his back was turned. He was prone to bouts of red-facedness and got out of bed on the wrong side every single day. He was a follower of the "drumming some sense into you" philosophy, for those of us less able to absorb his teaching. He was probably a very good teacher and was not disliked. Entering the short passageway brought the regulation half-tiled, half-eau-de-nil painted walls into view; presumably tiles were easier to clean – after grubby fingers had been trawled along their surface – than emulsion or distemper (a condition more usually to be found in dogs).

40

Along one wall was a double row of coat hooks sufficient to accommodate the outer clothing of the whole village population, and their relatives past and present. Placed at an unreasonable height on the side of the passage, these were employed for swinging on, an innocuous pastime indulged in by most children, but not without a price sometimes. My best pal's next older brother had a fatal accident in this pursuit, fracturing his skull in the process. The odds must be huge against such an event occurring. The infants' cloakroom was in the kitchen passageway around the corner.

Two doors on the right (one of which was an enthusiastic finger trapper owing to an ill-tempered spring return mechanism) admitted one into the main hall and assembly room. The main hall housed the stage, for plays, re-creations of the Nativity and concerts. Two long, faded, blue curtains often concealed the stage and led to speculation about what was hidden behind them. On one occasion I was more concerned about who or what was hidden under the stage, something creaked loudly and it wasn't the teacher or me. The single door to the left gave entry to the infant classes and sight of the Church clock through the window, if the door was open. Clock-watching doesn't interest small children. Older children like to know how much time has to pass before playtime; visits to the toilet increased as lessons progressed.

A stone staircase attached to the outer wall led to the first and only floor, which had two rooms one of which could only be entered by first passing through the other. Access was from the end of a balcony, which (apart from accommodating waiting children) was useful for dropping toffee papers and the occasional stink bomb on people's heads, to make the place reek of rotten eggs and cause the paper shop to be tuppence richer.

On the ground floor again the infant cloakroom led onto the kitchen, a small, two-sink enclave, and beyond that were the cellar steps.

I have no recollection of the cellar's contents and no one ever told me what was contained therein, suffice it to say that I respected Brian Butterworth's opinion that our best interests would not be served if we went down there, owing to the proximity of the graveyard and bogeymen just beyond the wall.

Paper-dart making was a common practice especially when the answer to a written question did not come immediately to your head.

The idea was to take a school pen-nib, break off the points, leaving two sharper points, crack the other end of the nib, using your desk lid, insert into the fracture a flight made from folded paper, and whiz it at the very high ceiling, there to stay until the long-suffering caretaker had enough to fill a small bucket. Someone (probably he) also had to clean or paint the ceiling periodically because it also was a target for ink pellets. Ink pellets are (or were) bits of folded paper generously soaked in a vicious, viscous powder-and-water concoction laughingly called "school ink". Apart from its willingness to blot your manuscript the ink had a habit of blocking your Platignum fountain pen and seeped into any dry wood or text-book whenever it was freed from its inkwell.

A more unlikely substance for the gentle art of calligraphy you will never find.

The use of ink pellets was common. Much favoured was the practice of whizzing one at the ceiling with a wooden ruler and hoping it stuck first time. If it did, there it would stay until it dried out and fell on a hapless individual in a later lesson, scaring them witless. If it didn't stick, in all likelihood it would fall near the teacher. A quick hand inspection would reveal the culprit. If you happened to be a bit sloppy around ink you also stood accused. I never indulged in these activities myself of course; the school was already full of kids far more able than I.

One of the Taylor boys from the bread shop indulged in this unsociable pastime. He was a couple of years older than the children in our class, and merit-worthy because of it. We were allowed to witness retribution in the shape of hand warming via the strap on skin method, after prayers but before register one morning. It was also interesting to watch him walk back to his place because of the violent hand flapping that followed this leathering. When seated, pressing the wounded extremity into the groin seems to have a soothing effect if accompanied by a screwed up, pain-racked face. Holding your breath helps as well. On the subject of register or roll call, names were called in alphabetical order. Anticipating the calling of your name was forbidden, not answering was also forbidden, even if you were absent it must have been forbidden because your name was called again. If your seat was empty then conclusions could be drawn.

The register was also called in the afternoon just in case you decided to emigrate during lunch.

The only permissible answer was "Yes, miss/sir". "Here!" or "Yo!" or anything "futuristic", was liable to provoke punishment. There were instances of smaller children instantly dozing off when their bottoms touched their seats. The art of responding to your name under these circumstances has never been mastered so far as I know.

The two younger junior classes were taught in the main hall separated by long screens made from polished wood mounted on small roller castors at each end, and fitted to the cross-members also at each end. They were ideal for riding on when they were being pushed back against the walls after lessons, making a rumbly, grumbly kind of noise during the operation – very much like the noise in your cuffed head if you were caught in the act. Chairs and desks were stacked in front of the screens to make room for morning "prayers and singing". I can't think why the morning service was given that name, maybe assembly was too fine a word for a small village school.

One of the two headmasters we experienced during our early learning stint was named Mr Hilton, he was a cricketer at Werneth CC and a vigorous slogger of the bowling in the school yard; one of those bounding men, a bit like a Doberman dog, you never knew where he would bound next. He led the singing each morning with great gusto and feeling, beating the air with his long arms. The only wisdom I can recall him imparting to us was "Sit up straight lad when I'm talking to you", I suppose you might hear better when upright but more than likely your head was nearer to the point of connection with the swinging hand of chastisement.

On religious occasions, Mr Calderley the vicar would appear in School, and say a few words, after which we all followed him from School round to the Church. In doing so we passed two very large stone tombs, memorials to the village benefactors, the Mellodews. They were surrounded by heavy-gauge, cast-iron, black-painted fencing with pointed bits strategically placed. Discussion took place about the use of the fences. It was not profound enough to make Darwin or Einstein fret. Most of the theories revolved around keeping us out or "them" in at night. Maybe to keep the Germans out as well, we being small and the War still fresh in people's memories.

To return to singing. Mrs Wrigley (or "Winnie" when she was out of earshot) accompanied us vigorously on the piano in our vocal efforts during assembly. She was short and sturdy with beautiful, wavy, shoulder length hair and the reddest lipstick I ever saw. When angry, which was often, she was in a class of her own, to coin a phrase. What a tartar! She could blister paint.

43

We rounded off assembly uttering prayer words near enough to the originals. Some of the children opted for the goldfish approach to the proceedings; lips moving, no sound coming forth. It's a fact that quite a bit of window-gazing went on, with the odd child dozing on its feet. Often a small voice carried on singing and then trailed off in embarrassment, when the rest of us had finished. There would be bouts of sniggering and feet shuffling, and depending on the disposition of the nearest teacher, you might hear a hefty smack followed by "pay attention boy" bounding around the rafters. If it was a girl, there might be a raised eyebrow or an "eyes-to-the-sky" sigh.

Love walked into my life around this time in the shape of Jean Morton. Well not exactly love, more an interesting occurrence. The young lady was a year older than I and was therefore a denizen of the other side of the aforesaid screen dividers. Suffering from some sort of temporary insanity she elected to write me a note which said rather pointedly, "David, I love you do you love me, Jean" – nothing else.

It passed through the screens surreptitiously and plopped onto my desk like a small hand grenade.

The only Jean in the next class up was the lady in question, and so, coming from a long and distinguished line of Lotharios and also being aged eight, I wrote on the back, in my best block capitals, "YES I DO" and pocketed it where it lay undisturbed along with bits of string, the odd badge, a few marbles and whatever "tab" (cigarette) cards I was saving at the time. There are revelatory times in your life and this was one of mine.

My mother in washing or patching my short trousers found the declaration and thought I should give it to Jean, so I did.

The young lady, exhibiting monumental indifference, crumpled it up and threw it away.

I was scarred for life, reputation shot before I'd acquired one.

The loss was made worse by the fact that she was a highly-desirable young lady. Her parents owned a sweet shop-cum-store at Strinesdale before they moved on and she was lost to all.

Whether toffees would ever have come my way it is impossible to know, I could have basked in the aura attached to a toffee shop owner's daughter though.

At about this time in a boy's life, the word "stupid" makes itself known, gets a regular airing and applies pretty much to anything extra-curricular that he does.

The word seems to be used to add extra impetus to the beating hand of discipline, when a boy is caught transgressing.

Entertaining activities like climbing school drainpipes, attempting to throw tennis balls over the Church roof, carving your initials in the school desk, seeing who could pee the highest up the school wall and unusually, leaded windows, called forth the adjective.

For those not familiar with leaded-window stripping, there is extreme pleasure in unravelling the thin, criss-crossed strips without having to snap any because you started in the wrong place. When one is small and untroubled, one places the tip of one's tongue between one's teeth, assumes a thoughtful expression and starts to unravel. It's dead simple.

There is extreme pain associated with this recreation if the windows are still in use. It might be concluded that there were legions of people just waiting to smack us about the head on a regular basis. I used to think there was an agreement between adults and their hands only to wave them in my direction. I was a fairly deft ducker and weaver in my prime.

In some religions, the acceptance of forthcoming pain is considered to be a virtue. It is a point of view that I don't subscribe to. Pain can only be so for those who have suffered it, not for those about to get it. I had occasion, along with PAB, to gouge my initials into a stone window ledge in the school yard. This laborious task necessitated the use of a very sharp nail and a stone the size of a grapefruit. Tongue protruding was an option not to be taken lightly; a cuffed head leads to a bitten tongue. I recall punishment being administered. Our letters were newly-carved amongst the old ones from previous generations. We didn't have the wit to rub dirt into the letters.

PAB never flinched from the strapping; he was a hard man. My approach to punishment was simple. Hold your hand out, shut your eyes, shut everything, listen for descending swish of cowhide. Yelp.

Withdrawing your hand at the moment of impact was fun for the observers because the teacher invariably hit his or her own leg. It is a natural reaction to withdraw your hand; perhaps it's a form of protest? The withdrawee however, could expect double punishment. A visit to the scene of the crime recently revealed that sandblasting had cleaned the building. "PAB" is still in evidence, "DL" only faintly outlined. "PAB" was staying. During those teacher/pupil hostilities parental approval was never sought when punishment was doled out.

45

There was never leave of appeal. Tut! The very thought!

Appealing is what kittens are, and cricketers do.

At senior school some years later, a certain amount of ingenuity was applied to the business of punishment. To make sure he never missed your outstretched palm, one teacher supported the underneath of your hand with a cane in his left hand, while thrashing away with his right. Another had strips of thin leather known as "the cat" (as in "o' nine tails"). There was no escape from the cat, it had a wide, fan-type action and wound round your hand a couple of times. Another teacher had a cross-member from the legs of a chair; it was like thick dowelling. Holding all your fingers in a bunch, he tapped their ends at the fingernail with the wood. It hurts and there is no evidence of oppression. Less hurtful forms of punishment were the strips of canvas used by a couple of female teachers, the strips were two inches wide by twelve inches long and a quarter of an inch thick. I had no idea what their former use was and I didn't want to know. One chap had a "rosy-ear club", a form of mental aggression. When classes were exchanging at the end of a particular period or lesson, a number of boys would emerge sporting a "rosy ear". The teacher grabbed the offending pupil in a headlock and vigorously rubbed the individual's ear until it glowed. It remained in this condition for a long time. Some lads wore the ear like a badge of courage. The same teacher would ask you to kneel on the floor and lift you upright by the short hairs to the front of your ear, all good harmless fun.

These days, the guardians of our morals would sue the teacher out of his birthright.

On spring mornings, in the retiring moon's washy afterglow, as the breeze gently stirs in the graveyard trees, and the low rising sun catches hold of the north windows, highlighting their coloured glass frescos and making our beautiful church come alive ... when, after your stone-kicking slow-meandering walk down the lane from home, subconsciously absorbing the distant drone of a propeller-driven engine aircraft ... when your main preoccupation is making the holes in your pockets bigger, sniffing, and keeping your dinner money out of the toffee shop's till ... when pulling your knee-length socks up is a strenuous exercise rather than a simple act of tidiness, and the thought of carrying on walking to Lands End (wherever that is) is flittering about in the far recesses of your mind ... when, unnoticed, the golden enchanter has slipped away from your dreaming hour, and a steam train hoots in the near distance along the Beal Valley bottoms ... when the School's roof and upper windows come into view above the ridged copings along the Grafton Street wall and negotiating the road's potholes turns into a game similar to hop flag ... then, my friends, the world is a wonderful place.

Sometimes after these events the world may stand still and you will hear the sharp exhalation of breath, along with the door-catch click of marbles in play.

For all these things to happen you have to be aged eight or so, almost late for school, and living in the late 'forties or early 'fifties. You also need to have arrived at the "merp" pitch, or the grounds in front of the Village Institute, in full possession of all your marbles. The Institute was situated directly opposite the main schoolyard gates and perhaps twenty yards back. All wood and windows, the building was a long cabin with concrete steps to the front entrance and was a tribute to the industrious efforts of our forefathers.

We children didn't know the building's purpose and I suspect that most – myself included – didn't care.

Much window-ledge hanging took place, in an effort to ascertain the building's contents; pointless really because the curtains were always drawn together. The building sat grimly aloof overlooking the marble pitch, impregnable in its tar-coated cladding. If PAB – an adventurer in the time-honoured mould – elected, along with anyone he could coerce, to climb the building, a disembodied voice from one of the Grafton Street back yards (usually Arthur Leyland's at the end house) a one-time workmate of mine, would issue instructions and advise in the following manner "Climb down and be quick about it". Because instructions to children have to be visual as well as vocal, deafness occurred fairly frequently. "I'll tell your father/mother," had a much weightier thrust to it. It did in my case anyway.

However, when you're young there is always a windmill to tilt at, the Don Quixote strain seems to run through most little boys.

The marble pitch was a hard, soil-and-cinder-covered area with holes that varied in size from the depth of a teacup to the depth of a small bucket. The small holes were for marble players of my class who might scrape together a dozen or so "merps", the large holes for the merp moguls. These kids had all their pockets full, jacket and pants, sometimes their cap and even an auxiliary marble bag. Full trouser pockets made the marble kings look a bit bulgy (like ferrets

47

playing in jodhpurs) when their owners were loaded up and mobile. "Holey" was the game for the big boys and would attract fifty marbles each per game. The distance from the bucket-sized hole was decided by mutual agreement, the idea being that the player tossing most marbles into the hole got first go at index-finger sliding the non-holed marbles to join the rest in the hole. If a marble fell short or went past the hole, the other player took his turn to do the same until the "alleys" were all in the hole. During the game, the strategy – especially if you were losing – would be to stand on the marble farthest from the hole, so that the marble sank into the pitch a bit and kick one away from the hole while no one was looking. My favourite ploy was dropping an extra marble from my pocket some distance from the hole. Nobody ever counted up after the game. If they did, they could usually be distracted around eighty-five or so by joining in the count on a different figure. Marbles had values in the same way as coins. An "ironnert" would be a steel ball-bearing from the mill. Their value would be highest – say six – because they were indestructible. A clay marble would be lowest in value, say one. One ironnert therefore equalled six clays. All values were in "erts"; two "erts", four "erts" and so on. Some had fixed "erts". Bull's-eyes were two "erts", new and very pretty marbles were "erted" by agreement. There were dobberts, alleys and beauts. I never got the hang of their value. I'm reminded of marble "erts" when I consider the "Euro" coin saga, worth whatever to whoever. A kid who had won a lot of "ironnerts" could easily be spotted because he was lopsided as he trundled around, one side of his elasticated braces stretched to pinging length.

I have a feeling the pitch was called "the barrens" because nothing grew there except tempers. It was a bit of a battleground where kids settled their differences. PAB was particularly good at this "fistic" pastime. Another game we played was "Wall-y". Two kids kicking a tennis ball against Leyland's gable end; good when they were out, not good otherwise. "Tag" and "Touch rugby" were others. Some un-athletic kids used to dig, the Lord only knows what they expected to find. "Eureka!" was a word unfamiliar to me until I found the Savoy dancehall awash with girls on rock 'n' roll nights.

Everyone should make a point of watching junior school football, twenty little boys running around a pitch in drifts like ants on a hot plate, being keenly observed by three people – two "goalies" and the referee. We played our home matches at Strinesdale, which was a pitch (mainly consisting of mud) that sank in the middle and ran parallel to a barbed-wire fence, surrounding Armitage's farm. A senior team, from the Strinesdale estate, used the pitch; the team was a very good side in those days. Those delegated to retrieve the ball from beyond the fence at these matches did so with great deliberation and not much obvious enthusiasm. The game consisted mainly of short bursts of kicking, elbowing and scrimmaging until some muddy kid burst out of the mêlée followed by the screaming pack. A bit like the Premier League really, without the pound coins of course, and footballers were classed as "foreign players" if they came from Saddleworth or Waterhead.

In the winter months, goal-scoring was easy because the goalie would be frozen to the spot. We've played on that pitch in blizzards, on ice with no visible lines, sometimes no visible goals, when smog descended upon us. By and large, in the cold stakes, it could have given Siberia a run for its money. There was a cup competition in the school league, the Clayton Cup, presumably donated by the same Clayton of "playing fields" fame. While walking to play these matches we sang a little ditty, "The Clayton Cup Rap" which went something like this:

> Roll along Moorside Rovers roll along.
> Put the ball in the net where it belongs.
> With a little bit of luck we'll win the Clayton Cup.
> Roll along Moorside Rovers roll along.

I've never supposed that anyone would want to claim copyright for that composition but you never know, do you? Someone tried to claim credit for a poem of mine once, and what's more he got paid for it. Blessed cheek!

Cricket took place opposite the football pitch, on the Moorside Cricket and Bowling facility. We occupied the western end of the ground, presumably because boys like to dig holes in the batting crease while waiting to be bowled out. In contrast to the football in winter, summers at Strinesdale were balmy, warm, sunny, insect-buzzing days. The mills could be heard humming in the village and there would be the occasional hum from the manure pile at Holroyd's farm. Most boys had only read the cricket manuals dedicated to "slogging" the ball. This they did with great fervour. We used wickets that sprang back up after being struck by the ball. They looked a bit like wobbling drunkards until they settled, awaiting the next onslaught. Bowling consisted mainly of approaching the bowling crease as fast as one could, aiming the "corky" ball in the general direction of the batsman and continuing to do this, until you were red-faced and knackered. This state of composure didn't occur if you bowled someone out however, the reinvigoration meter allowed you another five overs until your fuel tank ran dry. We kept the school cricket paraphernalia in the clubhouse in summer, returning it to school at the end of the season. The facts of junior cricket meant that the smaller batting pads wore out first, resulting in nine and ten year-olds wearing full-sized pads and wielding rather large lumps of willow. It was not uncommon to see a batsman with pads up to his waist peering round the edge of them trying to wield a bat bigger than himself, tripping up all over the place if invited to run between the wickets. We often played with cork balls which, having lost lumps of the crumbly stuff, did alarming things before hitting you about the ribs. There were no hip protectors or arm pads in those days, your protectors were your eyes and reflexes, and a "bouncer" was only trying to remove your head if he worked at the dancehall above Hillstores, chucking people out. Don't think bowlers didn't bowl fast forty or so years ago, they did – some very fast. It's just that the idea was to take wickets not maim somebody. The price for the modern game is low scores and "ripped off", disgruntled punters; this is partly reflected in the crowds which don't watch. I recently went to a youth match near my home. You would have thought they were playing for a trip to Brixton Prison; not a happy face amongst them, losing your wicket was trauma time. Their parents sat around like ghouls. In addition there was a one-man crowd and he insisted on bellowing phrases learned from the television and applauding the other side's mistakes. It's only a game, for goodness sake. Mr Hilton our headmaster at the time we played would have had a coronary at the very thought! A definition of the word "game" is "pastime"; maybe "game" belongs in the past. As the old saying goes, "If it ain't nailed to the vestry walls, it ain't sacred anymore".

In our final year at junior school, we were allocated two lessons on Thursday mornings, to become, or try to become, proficient at swimming. A number of us had already visited the public baths at Mortar Street, Hillstores on Saturday mornings with older kids, mainly because we thought we might be missing something. We were to be introduced to the correct method of propulsion in water by a professional instructor in the shape of Mr Cooper, an international performer. (That's an assumption because he had a Union Jack stitched on the front of his leotard-style bathing costume.) Mr Cooper was a well-rounded individual and his method of reassuring kids who thought they might drown, was to float on his side propping his head up with his arm and hand, while smoking a cigarette with his other hand. The display was effective, bearing in mind that he was so large in girth. All I knew was what I'd seen at the mill-lodge. Throw a large stone into water and it sinks without trace. I remember thinking at the time or maybe a bit later, that if his belly were punctured he would be off like a speedboat to the deep end of the baths. Mr Cooper was not to be trifled with. The initial lesson on the breaststroke took the form of his holding you across his large forearms on the water's surface, about two yards from the hand rail surrounding the plunge and swishing you towards the rail shouting: "Swim boy, swim". It didn't bother most of us who had some experience of the depth at the shallow end of the pool, but others newly-introduced to the idea did a bit of screaming and a heck of a lot of frenzied thrashing. My best pal for many years, Lawrie Turner, took to swimming like a duck takes to water and it gave him a position in the sporting fraternity. He never went much on football or cricket. We spent a lot of time shivering, carrying soggy towels and "cossies", getting earache and being unwell. The law of probability dictates that chlorine added to water will be swallowed in copious quantities for the duration of the lessons. We were encouraged to buy a cup of hot Bovril or Oxo after the lessons, particularly in winter. The evil brew swilling around in one's stomach, plus the stench from the slaughterhouse next door to the baths, resulted in a fair amount of retching on the way to the bus stop. If you were able to suppress the desire to vomit at this point, the swaying of the old Crossley bus grinding up Ripponden Road usually did the trick. Mr Cooper liked a cigarette during his teachings. He upheld Captain Webb the Channel swimmer, portrayed on the front of his matchbox, as someone to aspire to be. Although I like water – it's good for the garden – I was never going to emulate Captain Webb.

Other forms of exercise were PT (physical training) and dancing. Dancing I mustn't have enjoyed because I seem to have blanked it from my memory, probably regarding it as embarrassing, a girlie thing, prancing about hither and thither stuff. PT took place in various guises, all meant to keep you fit. Most of us were shaped like racing weasels anyway, so I could see little point. I looked up "Calisthenics" in the dictionary and it would describe our school's participation in an occasion known as "Spartakiada". I've sat in a corner with a blanket over my head and cannot come up with anything remotely resembling or appertaining to the name, except a Russian football club. The event took place at Watersheddings Rugby Ground. I vaguely remember it being a synchronised exercise or dance affair with kids from different schools all moving simultaneously in a set pattern, creating a living tapestry or tableau. I remember a practice session in which I or we didn't take part because I'm not synchronised, but observed with some embarrassment that some schools didn't "nise" with other schools' "synchro". The effect was similar to the one achieved by forcing a piece of jigsaw into a place where it won't fit. Anyway, they got it right on the day. There was probably a lot more to it than that but if I wasn't personally involved I had as much interest as a gourmet in a chip shop. Other occupations included the usual gymnastics, buck vaulting, cartwheeling, somersaulting (a name derived from Somerset ham-curers?) and running along benches commando style, which was fine if you had brought your black gym pumps for the occasion, disastrous if not. Stocking feet and polished benches are a bone-bruising duo, front teeth and oak floorboards made unscheduled contact on a few "outings" that I attended. It was all good practice for walking along the school wall. The copings, as previously stated, had a pointed spine along their whole length and were salt glazed, giving them a log-splitting sharpness to deter anyone from walking along the wall, or from escaping from the school yard while the gates were shut. Many attempts to walk the wall came to an abrupt end and may have affected child reproduction at a later stage in people's lives. The injuries were never as bad as refusing the "dare" though.

Pumps ("trainers" were men who shouted at jockeys) could be bought from school and were made from black canvas with a black rubber elastic cross strap and black soles. Lace-up pumps were more expensive, therefore classier. White pumps, worn mainly by the girls whose parents had a few bob, could be used. Keeping them white was an operation in itself. To apply the whitening, first wet the pump's canvas, then rub on white cream, either from a tube or a flat polish tin – a stick of whitening could be used but wasn't much good. Too liberal an application of whitening would, after the drying period, cause the pump to resemble a dried-up waterhole. After the first few steps, bits of dandruffy particles flirted in all directions. Too little of the application left the pumps a bit hung-over-looking, a queasy grey colour. If the whitening ran out halfway through the operation – well, that was tough. My sister was grievously and vocally upset when that happened. Our Jean had a world-class bottom lip and displayed it unashamedly if irritated. Dressing for PT was a bit of a lottery. Boys whose parents could afford it, wore shorts, the others, their ordinary short trousers. Girls wore navy blues and vests. The only name to adorn any of the apparel was your own. Money badges like *Nike* and

Puma hadn't appeared; pumas ran around America eating people. One refined young lady had to do PT in her semi-transparent, silk underwear, having forgotten her "gym" gear. The poor girl didn't know where to look. I suppose (which I do a lot) in those days there was an element of "that will teach you" in most unfortunate things. Should such an incident happen today "trauma" would feature in the ensuing conversation and a barrister would be hauled away from his three-hour-long lunch.

The ruggedness of our existence meant we were all fit, healthy and thereby equipped to meet one Olive Lawton, a gunslinger amongst teachers. Miss Lawton had been at the school for eons and cherished a seriously scary reputation. I'm sure that the good lady had many virtues but I can't name any. She lived in Haven Lane, which meant that we had to pass her house on our way to school. I know that if you enjoy a bad reputation, then other circumstances will qualify it. The house always looked dark and watchful, a bit like a tiger's lair, to be passed in a hurry and on the opposite side of the lane. My first memory of her is of a grey, elderly, slim person, who wore spectacles and dressed severely. She had braids tied or clipped to the top of her head and she was icily polite in class.

Miss Lawton had a strict punishment regime, not to be fallen foul of. To transgress in class was to invoke her wrath, and her method of chastisement was a byword, later to be passed into folklore. The offendees (usually older boys) might be asked to stand on a desk, which in her room had a long, black, wooden top with equally-spaced inkwells and a bench seat to accommodate half-a-dozen pupils. She would pull your woolly, knee-length socks down, which you'd just pulled up in anticipation of the event, and wallop your calf muscle with a wooden ruler, either leg would do. Up went the sock and you would be asked to recite the last two sentences she had spoken. By now you were incapable of speech of any kind and utterances came out in the form of a neolithic whine. You were, in addition, unable to accomplish this task because you were invariably up on the desk for talking not listening. The same treatment was then meted out to your other leg, which gave some sort of balance to the stinging effect.

Kids passed time in the playground comparing wounds by measuring the red welts to white skin ratio; sometimes the winner was chosen for his limping abilities. Miss Lawton chose to vacate the school premises and retire rather than clash with my form, which was lucky for her. PAB would probably have tested her patience right off the barometer, assuming that she had any of course. The lady would pass you in the village and say "hello" as if nothing had happened. Nobody bore a grudge (*somebody* must have). Crime and punishment, it was as simple as that. What a close-knit community we were.

My favourite teacher in the whole of my career at St Thomas's was Mrs Wrigley, lately deceased at the time of writing. I happened to meet her a couple of years ago in C&A in Oldham. She didn't recognise me but she hadn't changed much herself. She knew of my scribbling in *Lancashire Life* and various other magazines plus the *Oldham Evening Chronicle*, and seemed pleased to see me. As with most things, take someone out of a fixed situation and they become someone else. She wasn't the fearsome lady who taught our final year. Mrs Wrigley was wife to Harry who ran the village Post Office-cum-store, and mum to Christopher who was my sister's age – five years younger than I. She taught, up to eleven-plus standard, various subjects and she was proficient in all of them. The lady had a formidable temper. Who wouldn't have when some of us could boast only four brain cells? What we couldn't absorb was drummed into us by repetition, an educational method superior to the "let 'em learn in their own time" theory of recent years, which means that some don't learn at all. .

Mrs Wrigley was without doubt the biggest influence on our junior school lives from a learning point of view.

I can't resist a little smile to myself when I think how the politically-correct and the doom and gloom merchants of today would levitate at the mention of the old-fashioned methods. I have little faith in today's "happy clappy" indoctrination. Modern-day, computer-happy think-shrinks rule; the human touch seems to be disappearing. Perhaps one day the computer will welcome the pupils with "Good morning" and kick them out when they've worked through their educational program and never a teacher to be seen.

Whatever the polically-correct may say, my generation doesn't have too many "hang-ups" and we are certainly not the tortured souls they would make us out to be. The educational system worked for us. What price the psychiatrist's couch these days I wonder?

For those of us not encumbered by the need for blackboard cryptography, there were many more pleasant diversions in the school curriculum. We were marshalled together as a class on nice sunny days and taken for nature walks, often crossing Sholver Lane by Hartley's farm and proceeding through the meadows towards Besom

Hill reservoir. The fields had ponds for the livestock to drink from. They were host to frogspawn, tadpoles, newts, pond skaters (some kind of fly) that zipped around on the water's surface. If you touched one with a bulrush stem, they all scattered like chickens at Christmas. The pond nearest Hartley's farm had ducks on it, they steamed around like bickering old ladies on a day trip to Blackpool.

I'm not given to wearing rose-tinted spectacles very often, so to speak, but it is a fact that fields full of buttercups, kingcups, "mother die" (if you picked it your mother was supposed to die, there should have been a lot of dead mothers if that was the case) and thistle stretched as far as the eye could see, in mid-summer. Larks made homes in every field and flew into the sun never to come back. I found out later that they stop singing at the top of their flight and sink to earth in silence. Insect activity was tangible and butterflies were in abundance. Cabbage whites were quite large; Red Admirals were chased and caught often. We kept caterpillars in matchboxes on a piece of leaf; I'm not sure why, we just did. (Budding homebuilders?)

These days, sitting immovably across Hartley's fields, is Sholver Phase One development. This, I think, was built initially to house the residents of St Mary's ward who were being turfed out of their homes under that ill-conceived name "slum clearance" or to give it its proper title, Compulsory Purchase Order. Townspeople in such numbers were never going to be content, herded into the middle of a green desert and so it proved. In the meantime a beautiful village went down the tubes at a fair rate of knots. Somewhere within its sprawling environs, in quiet moments, if there are any, you may hear the village gulp as it keeps taking the aspirin, hoping its headache will go away. Sermon finished!

1. Haven cottage where David Lavisher grew up and dreamt the dreams of the innocent.
(Courtesy Mrs. J. Gledhill).

2. Mr. Bill Chapman, the farmer, his grandson Derek Beard and Derek's mother Lily.
(Courtesy Gordon Howard).

3. Above: St. Thomas's Church, Moorside, viewed from the site of the former Moorside Mill. *(Courtesy Mrs. J. Gledhill).*

4. Below: A very serious author waiting to be executed for his childhood crimes. *(Courtesy Sylvia Lavisher, who took this photo during a break from dusting insurance policies).*

5. A pre-war aerial picture of Mellodew's Mills, Moorside with Haven House, one of the homes of the Mellowdew family, at the top right. *(Courtesy Local Studies Library, Oldham M.B.C.).*

6. Moorside School in 1950. *Back row (l to r):* Sidney Hatch, Eric Wood, John Wright, Paul Blagborough, Eric Harding, Robert Mellor, Billy Kershaw. *Middle row (l to r):* David Lavisher, Alec Brookes, Peter Barber, Pat Wood, Pauline Blakeman, Brian Butterworth, Barry Simpson, Laurence Turner. *Front row (l to r):* Mary Davies, Marion Whitlock, Jennifer Brierley, Carol Grimshaw, Mary Hughes, Sheila Jackson, Betty Taylor. *(Courtesy of Betty Taylor).*

7. This photo at Moorside School was possibly taken in 1951 or 1952. The children appear to have gained weight after wartime food rationing had almost ended. *Back row:* Miss Taylor, John Wright, Paul A. Blagborough, Barry Simpson, Sidney Hatch, Derek Yates, *Middle row:* Alec Brookes, David Lavisher, Peter Barber, C. Stone, Pauline Blakeman, Pat Wood, Eric Harding, Brian Butterworth, Laurence Turner, *Front row:* Eric Wood, Marion Whitlock, Jennifer Brierley, Betty Taylor, Sheila Kay, Elaine Fenton, Sheila Jackson, Billy Kershaw. *(Courtesy Betty Taylor.)*

8. Still looking as if butter wouldn't melt in their mouths a couple of years later. David Lavisher is now second right on the middle row with PAB next to him. *Back row (left to right):* Brian Butterworth, Eric Harding, Peter Barber, Alec Brookes. *Middle row (l to r):* Sidney Hatch, Laurence Turner, Pauline Blakeman, Pat Wood, Kay Forrest, David Lavisher, Paul Blagborough. *Seated (l to r):* Eric Wood, Marion Whitlock, Sheila Kay, Elaine Fenton, Betty Taylor, Billy Kershaw. *Front pair (l to r):* John Wright, Derek Yates. Moorside School in 1954. *(Courtesy of Betty Taylor).*

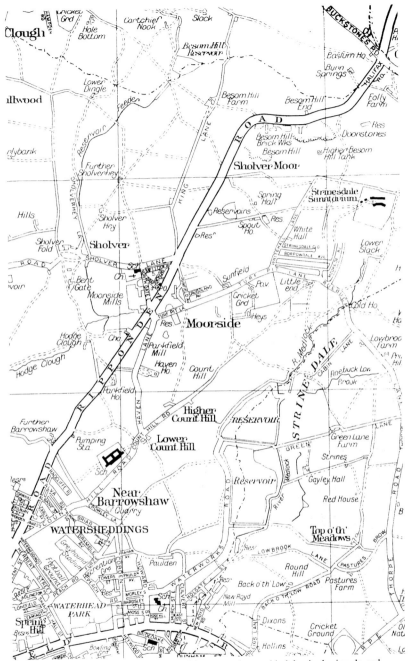

9. The Moorside area – big enough for children to explore and indulge in derring-do and other time-consuming activities. (*Courtesy Geographia, Ed. J. Burrows & Co. Ltd., London*).

Sholver Green

Sholver Green was a dice-throw of houses, plus Howard's farm and the Pullet Inn, now The Northgate. Gordon Howard one of three sons and a similar age to me, married into my wife's family, which is a tribe really, spreading out around the globe as it does. He and his brother David now hold the fort at the Chadderton Heights pub.

The village gave shelter to four public houses, and one Conservative club. How The Pullet Inn ever made ends meet, being situated in the middle of nowheresville, I can't imagine. Maybe you had to grab the passing trade and pull it in. My Uncle James was a paperboy in the village and part of his Saturday evening round was delivering the Green Final in Sholver. After he had delivered it to The Pullet Inn, the chap named Fletcher in the adjacent house used to beckon him across and check his pools coupon from the next paper in James's bag before giving it back. James then delivered it to Spencer's further down the lane. Whether James was the recipient of any winnings, or got the odd toffee, isn't clear. Things were tight in those days, so make up your own mind about that one.

A sunny afternoon excursion would be to Peacote, down Sholver Lane, skirting "The Green" past Howard's farm and over the footbridge. If you carried on you came to Wilkes Street, if you turned right you came to Peacote, a marshy stretch of land heading for Heyside. The area contained toads, dragonfly, marsh flowers and puddles of mud. Covered in bulrushes and reeds it had no discernible path, which meant we could play hunt the shoe if someone stepped into the quagmire. A crepe-soled sandal offered the most or best entertainment when eventually found. Even-paced walking provided a squelch-flop effect until the mud set. Those lighter of foot offset the tedium of walking by hopping between cowpats and the cart track, to and from school. The less agile carried the consequences of their failed endeavours around all day and were referred to as "stinky" whatever their name was.

Peacote could only be attempted in high summer because of the nature of the place. Afternoons and hot sun were the pre-requisites.

I've always been a bit of a loiterer (not with intent) and I know I've said it before, but I can remember leaning on the fence in the blistering heat, looking at Howard's farm and hearing it tick in the stillness. No rhythm, just a hot, slow tick.

The Queen

We had not been left Moorside School long, October 1954, to be exact, when the Queen of England and everywhere else at that time, fed up with living amongst the rich and famous, decided one rainy day to come and look us up. The school was closed while we presented our flag-waving selves for inspection on Rochdale Road, Oldham, just after St Domingo Street and next to a shop at the top of Middleton Road which, when the Queen wasn't passing, sold second-hand clothes displayed on hangers outside the premises. It could have been a pawnshop. The Queen and the Duke of Edinburgh drove past and on a command from teacher we all waved and yelled and that was it. We got a beaker commemorating the event and a small, square, plastic "thingy" with thin perpendicular lines on it, the precursor of the hologram. Turned one way a picture of the Queen appeared, turned the other, Prince Philip. Magic! Pokemon and Playstation aren't in the same league as entertainment, as you can tell. On such small tokens a lifetime of fealty is built. We didn't know the difference then, between a monarchy and a republic because there wasn't any need to. Newspaper speculation these days provides an alternative viewpoint. Anyway, whatever the advantage of either contention, Philip Mountbatten is my kind of guy; the old maxim "like it or lump it" is appropriate here.

I once worked with a chap who thought the Queen's money should be appropriated and shared out amongst all her subjects. When I said I thought we might get 10 per cent of one penny each, he, not being mathematically minded, said, "That would do". Mind you, he also thought that a ploughman's lunch was charged to a farmer's expense account and therefore tax deductible.

Wintertime

In wintertime we never asked to go and look at the snow. People today jump into their cars and go to ogle a few inches of slush. The snow came to look at us. It came in joyous, copious quantities and lay around in frosty stubbornness for a long time. In its initial curiosity it sneaked under doors, fastened itself to school windows and peered in from the roof troughs as icicles. The roads were filled in up to five feet or so and if the wind came during the process, eight- or nine-foot-high drifts were common on higher ground. Counthill was higher ground but that didn't stop our mother from battling down Haven Lane, or more likely, the fields, to go to work in the mill. Time lost was money lost. Today you get on your "mobile" which is permanently glued to your hand and tell your employers that snow has been forecast in Doncaster and you won't be coming to work today.

If snow came during a school day, which it must have done, the teachers were concerned about the kids who lived in the outlying districts of Grains Bar, Strinesdale and beyond, and about us Counthillians. Up to a foot deep wasn't considered a cause for concern and in my case, one hundred yards down the lane my mother was slogging away in the mill so I wasn't concern-worthy.

In one of our junior years, our class was seated looking out towards the gable end house in Northgate Lane, addressed as "Sholver Lane/Mellodew Street", back-to-back houses. When I was "teachered up", which was usually five minutes after the lesson started, if I wasn't dozing off I spent some time counting the rows of bricks on the gable end house. Because of this mathematical practice I was always amongst the first to see the snowflakes drifting past the windows. Word soon spread and everyone but the teachers knew the score, having their backs to the windows and all. Telling teacher about the weather was an option preferably taken up by a girl. If a boy mooted the fact, he invited censure, the principle being if he wasn't listening he wasn't learning. Whispered discussions among those of us who lived in the outback were centred upon how deep the snow would get before 4 pm. The fervent hope would be that at about 3 pm, or "playtime" as the fifteen-minute break was known, there would be enough snow to justify our abandoning ship.

Snow attacked the village with great relish; from no snow to no village was the norm. It was better if we had snow at night. Often the drifts would be three quarters of the way up the terraced houses. The men used to dig out their doorways, giving the impression of cave entrances. Dig out in the morning, off to work, and dig out again before re-entry at night. Some digger-outers would throw the snow in the lane and the wind would gleefully seize the opportunity to create an impassable drift across the lane. These people were worshipped by us and cursed by the milkmen, coalmen, postmen *et al.*

I have retained in memory a conversation between my parents some years ago, about a chap who was walking down Turf Pit Lane from Strinesdale past the cricket field. The snow had drifted across the lane. In those days the footpath wasn't built and it was just a lane with a boundary wall to the cricket field and a boundary wall to Hartley's field. A number of men were walking along the field wall, the lane being impassable, when one of them slipped and vanished into a drift for a short while before they hauled him out and carried on in the morning darkness to their work. He was snowed under with work that day I guess.

My mother remembers that in her childhood sledging took place down Sholver Lane to The Pullet Inn – a long pull back up to go down again. She also said that the inhabitants of Sholver Green who had dealings with horses and carts were not pleased about the sledging. Polished cobbles and iron-shod hooves aren't conducive to making vehicular progress. Horses had sacking tied to their feet sometimes to give adhesion and some horseshoes were spiked or hobnailed.

From Counthill our sledging track was the footpath between Highfield Terrace – known as Hill 60 (presumably named after a battle, bitterly fought, over a hill at Flanders during the First World War) and the end house adjoining The Highfield Inn, then owned or run by a classmate's parents, he being Barry Simpson. "Willing" is a good word to describe Barry, he was a nice lad. The pub was a flag-floor affair, dark and gloomy during the day with that wonderful, washy, beery, damp smell. An empty pub to me was like an empty church. Waiting for something or somebody. You know the kind of thing, hallowed or hollowed, secretive.

The footpath doesn't exist any more. It ran from Ripponden Road to Counthill Road, ending at the side of Alice Mills's house. It was interrupted by two "stealos" at the two fields' boundaries. These were actually stiles, which Fred Scholes, a chronicler of Moorside at the beginning of the last century refers to as "steal holes". Holcombe View Close now sits astride the path and doesn't look as if it's about to move to let anyone pass by.

In the field to the rear of Alice Mills's at Counthill Road and next to the footpath, was a caravan of the Romany gypsy type. It had four wheels, was made of lacquered wood, the traditional bow roof and stovepipe, and three steps leading to the double doors. The area immediately surrounding the dwelling was covered with stove ash. The lady occupant was known as "Monie" and was happy with her own company. Billy Kershaw and I used to sit under the caravan listening to her talk to herself, so she must have been. I have no recollection of her chasing us off with a broom, or whatever old ladies did to remove pests at that time. I don't know who she was in relation to the nearby population. Whether she upped and "took boggart" (ran off – unfettered) or expired even, I was not in a position to know. How the caravan got into the field is also a bit of a riddle, the only vehicular access being a gateway next to Mrs Whitehead's house, with no road into the field, unless you consider a three yard square patch of knee deep mud, a road. The field was used to keep hens and had three long, cabin-type, hen houses with enough Rhode Island Reds to make feather pillows for the whole of the English aristocracy. Mills's allowed the farm bull to graze in the field and enjoy the sunshine, if he'd been a good lad and not squashed anybody recently. A yard-long spike was driven into the ground and he was tethered by his nose ring and three yards of chain to the spike. We were never encouraged to stroke the bulls or offer them anything other than advice. The average nine-year-old boy could be tossed into the air a long way before returning to the ground. Maybe that's where the expression "I'm over the moon" came from.

Continuing with snow. On a good day or evening, and Ripponden Road blocked with snow, there was enough acceleration on a sledge going down to clear the road and shoot out into Frank Hough's meadow over the wall. Not for the faint-hearted or the sane. I remember that it was better done in an evening, when the sledging track had iced over and was faster. The plummeting could be ten to fourteen feet, depending on the drift size over the wall. There were a number of good plummeters of whom I wasn't one. The Taylor lads from the bread shop were keen aerial tobogganers. Malcolm in particular was keen on anything that should have carried a hazard warning notice.

Deep snow, for obvious reasons, rounds off the edges of things, dimming focus and making contrasts softer. Smoke-blackened stone mills become less overpowering clad in wind-blasted snow. A soft yellow light shone out of their opaque windows; perhaps the snow's reflection affected the otherwise harsh brightness. There was no sense of brooding watchfulness under a good dose of the white stuff. The Church, attractive at the best of times, looked even better under snow, straight off a Christmas card. All the nooks, crannies and angular outcrops and the oblique roof sections used to be filled in with snow. Reflected light created a kind of stillness as if the place was sleeping. (Why churches have to have chunks of stone and ridges, where ridges aren't needed, is a bit of a puzzle. I accept the idea of distinctive design, or visual impression, but why did they need to "overdo" their appearance? In most places the church building dwarfed the surrounding properties anyway.) Depending upon the type of snow – large snowflakes stuck together was better than the powdery stuff – we could roll it into big boulders, for making snowmen or big barricades in the narrow lanes, causing any traffic unfortunate enough to be negotiating the lane, to stop.

When a driver thus detained was leaving his vehicle to establish where the massive snowballs had come from, and to discover the culprits, he would be generously peppered with small snowballs. It was usually a pastime enjoyed by older lads and I innocently on-looked from a safe distance. One criterion had to be met – that you didn't know the unfortunate driver, and more to the point, that he didn't know you. Fine sifting snow usually meant hard frosts, which also meant the making of slippy kerries or slides. For some unknown reason, the best ones were made outside the front door of a particularly nasty person's house and were quite lethal, especially if the street lamp on the footpath had gone out (through failure or otherwise). The person who was the object of such attentions would be sure to cause amusement by a bit of running on the spot or pavement cruising and you could guarantee the odd swear word from somewhere in the dark. It was unfortunate that blameless neighbours were sometimes caught out as well. No one got sued and the worst punishment, if you were found out, was a smack round the ear.

A much enjoyed recreation was the displeasing sight of the Council gritting squads and the booing plus pelting of snowballs at the unfortunate stalwarts as they went about their business. The vehicles travelled slowly – maybe ten miles an hour at most – salt having to be hand-shovelled into a hopper, dropping onto a spinning plate before distribution over the roads, and so the teams were vulnerable to the odd bombardment.

The snowballing line-up was a bit like the old rifle brigades, one line fired while the other reloaded. With us however it was free fire. The fleetest of foot threw close up to the enemy operation, the more restrained throwers a little further back, and the young or weight-distressed contented themselves with hitting the fleet of foot because they stood too far back to reach the objects of our wrath.

The target's chosen defence (of descriptive abuse) was inadequate retaliation compared to the might of the flung snowball.

Snow came at Christmas now and again. Once, very confidently and aged six, I ran outside in full cowboy gear; guns, hat, jacket and "chaps" (leg protection against the chaparral, which, so far as I know doesn't grow at Counthill) football boots and football. Ploughing through a foot of snow in the field at the back of Billy Kershaw's house at Counthill, I was watched by a window-full of bemused Kershaw kids. Billy was my pal so any scorn heaped on me was, er, tolerable, just. We reminisced about the occasion later. Bill passed away recently; he was an integral part of my childhood.

Christmas came one year in the shape of a full-sized bike with 26 inch wheels and 1¼ inch wide tyres, a 23 inch frame, its own stand, dynamo lights, curved wing nuts, silver pump, it was the bee's knees. Charlie Spencer, four years my senior, inspected it and declared it to be his old one which had been done up, re-painted etc. I didn't care as long as he didn't want it back. I loved that bike, it was my passport to paradise and it got me a long way from my father, which suited us both.

Riding along Northgate Lane, absorbed in watching the tyre tracks behind me unwinding in the newly fallen snow, brought contact with a parked car. One of those big black, solid wheel, twelve-inch chromium headlight things with the kind of bumper you now see on lorries. They seemed to glare at you, inviting you to test your bones against their ton-and-a-half implacability. My ten-year-old bones weren't even going to frighten the paintwork. The bike didn't do much better either. Suffice to say that the bike was undamaged and my skin clung to my frame without any leaks.

Since that incident, I have spent as little time looking behind me as possible. The coughing roar of an angry lion, or the whingeing of traffic police sirens on the motorway, might cause me to sneak a backward glance and only then if they haven't passed me within a few seconds. If car manufacturers knew that driving mirrors on my cars are for adornment purposes only they would leave them off altogether. Being at the front means I don't have to see who's coming up behind me. There have been times when my licence has looked like a crib board because of conscientious policemen, wringing the last ounce out of their car engines to catch me. What the heck! If you drive in the slow lane you get run over by a truck. "You plays, you pays", as they say.

When I was quite small I was told snow went back to Lapland when we'd finished with it. When I asked Sofie, my wife's six-year-old granddaughter, where it went, she looked at me as if I was unhinged and said, "Down a grid".

The little fibs we absorbed quite happily as children won't wash with today's kids.

People and Places

Because of the mills, small businesses thrived in the village and were concentrated on Ripponden Road. From the Watersheddings end on the right-hand side, were The Highfield Inn, Bull's Head, Waggon and Horses, and Bob Berry's butchers which sat halfway between first and last. The address may have been Turf Pit Lane, I'm not sure. Entrance to the premises was through a half door and then a full door. The half door was closed in summer, presumably to stop dogs snaffling the strings of sausages hanging around the shop. The loud clicking of the half-door latch produced Bob from the depths of the building. He was clad from shoulder to knee in white attire, fronted by the traditional blue and white striped apron. He also wore a black eye patch, which made him look like a very clean pirate. The image was made more realistic by his sharpening of his cutting knife on the poker-like "steel", as he approached the counter to serve a customer. If you went to the shop later in the day his apron would be covered in gore. To a boy with my imagination his knife sharpening took on a different significance. If I stuck my head over the half door to see who was in the shop, he always had a friendly word. A friend of my mum's and also my godmother, Joan Fullard, says that Bob used to give a glacier mint to each of his customers. Fancy me not remembering a source of free toffees.

On the left hand side of Ripponden Road from the same end, was the garage. On the outside left-hand wall was a large sign saying FILL UP FOR THE MOORS. Running my under-used imagination up to speed in my later years, I wondered if they were the same Moors who inhabited the beautiful, romantic Alhambra Palace at Granada, Spain.

Maybe the Moors family had fallen on hard times. Filling up for the Moors wasn't necessary at the garage; there was a petrol pump at the Junction Inn, Denshaw, on the corner of the building. It was still there when I was in my late teens, although unused by then.

On the opposite side of the road from the garage was a water installation, which gave its name to the garage and the area around the bus stops. It was called "the pumping station". The next shop was the "cloggers", a cobbler's shop known in the village as "Yeddons" regardless of the fact that it was owned by Harold Chapman (not related to the paper-shop man). The premises are now 603 Ripponden Road and have reverted to being a house. What the present occupants would think of the likes of me sitting in their front room waiting for my clogs to be ironed or shoes "solely heeled" (soled and heeled) I can't imagine. There was a form provided to sit on, in my case to stand on, watching the cobbler beat the daylights out of the footwear. There was a peculiar clunking sound when the iron was being nailed to a wooden clog base. If you are on the tallish side (as I am) and have spent a lifetime walking into low doorways and ceiling beams, you will know the sound.

Apprenticed to Harold Chapman in my childhood was Maurice Buckley from Grafton Street, who had a brother called Donald. Maurice played cricket for Moorside, Werneth and Oldham, ending his career umpiring in the Saddleworth League and was on my admiration list. I spent endless hours watching the likes of Roy Arundale, Norman Clafton, Maurice Udall and Maurice Buckley, playing in the long, hot summers. I have half a mind that Uncle James was a willow-to-leather man at Moorside also.

The side of the clogger's shop boasted hoardings with the original Bisto Kids and Craven 'A' advertisements. At the other end of that block, opposite the Highfield Inn, there was a full-length advert for Bile Beans, a small black pill for making your innards happy to be inside your outtards. By coincidence there was a boy called Billy Bean who lived in the same row as the advert. Famous and he never did anything!

Mrs Smith's shop came next, directly opposite the bottom of Alexandra Terrace. It was a corner-shop type place, selling a bit of everything: vegetables, cleaning materials, and other indispensable items. One of my less-celebrated initiatives occurred at Mrs Smith's shop.

It happened that I was despatched upon an errand to acquire some goods for our mother. A ten-shilling note was wrapped in a piece of paper upon which she had written the names of the items required. During the meandering dawdle that is usual for small boys on tedious errands, I must have decided to read the note (I was being clever) and memorised the items written down. I arrived at the shop and Mrs Smith appeared behind the counter. She was petite with dark, curly hair and a nice lady. I asked her for that which I thought mother required. Because I have the attention span of a very small gnat, the wrong items arrived at our house some time later. Our mother had a stamping do before dragging me off in a horizontal hurry to ask Mrs Smith what she was playing at. Mrs Smith protested that she hadn't seen a list of items. By now I was a bit jittery and said I'd given both notes to Mrs Smith. Mother demanded her money back and we bounced out of the shop like two ping-pong balls. Mrs Smith, who must have thought we'd escaped from somewhere, was totally bemused by the whole thing. My feet only touched the ground half-a-dozen times the length of Alexandra Terrace and I arrived home a long time before mother did. That short and much-loved phrase of the 1950s "showing me up" got a thoroughly good airing as I ducked around the room between clouts. I didn't go to Mrs Smith's for a long time afterwards. I bet she was more than pleased about that. Anyone who knows me will tell you that shopping is not what I'm good at.

Brooks's bakers and confectioners was at the other end of the row of terraced houses and the shop was numbered 623. It also, is now a domestic dwelling. Whether Brooks's or Yates's bakers were responsible for making the "box loaf" (a loaf without crust) I'm not sure.

The Brooks family engaged in a number of occupations, one of which was a painting and decorating business. One of the semi-detached houses in Haven Lane still bears the inscription to that effect at the side of the front door. It may be the original plaque that Edgar Brooks displayed over fifty years ago.

Next to the bakers came two modern terraced rows, all being numbered 625, with identifying letters A-K inclusive. On the pavement outside 625J was a post box, tallish with a domed top and no footholds, which made getting on top of it something of a mission. Staying there without Les Nuttall asking you to get down was a lifetime ambition. Les was a nice man and a very good sledger in winter down the Highfield's track with his daughter, who I think was also named Leslie.

There was a piece of open ground and then Conduit Street, before the next buildings which were two shops, the Co-operative store and next door the Co-operative butchers. You can only say so much about a butcher's shop. We never, ever shopped at the Co-op because mother said items were dearer, to pay for the "divi". When I asked her what "divi" was, if I remember correctly, she said, "Oh, shut up". Mother's way of explaining things wasn't up to much at times.

A few, low-windowed, modern terraced houses separated the Co-op from the Conservative Club, which is now The Village Inn, a pub. Fred, Mrs Buckley and daughter Mary lived in the end house adjoining the club. Fred was the club steward if memory serves me correctly.

When I was perhaps nine or so, mother made the three-tear (tier) wedding cake when Mary elected to marry a chap from Watersheddings named Denis Vernon. The tear bit is because one of the three tiers "caught" while being baked and we were forced to eat it, which meant mother had to make another one. When I say "forced", we were handcuffed, blindfolded and had guns pointed at us until it was all gone. Yeah! And Father Christmas was a chimney sweep.

I also had the pleasure of finger scouring the mixing bowl AGAIN. I look at Mary's wedding photos and see myself in brown tweed jacket, brown long trousers, shoes and tie to match, and wonder, who the heck is that? The wedding reception was upstairs at the Club, and the only other memory I have is of my sister dressed in green and white, being a bit standoffish, like a rabbit in a burrow at a lion park, because of her reticence in unfamiliar company.

She ain't like that now, and isn't to be messed with.

A chap named Ray kept the chip shop next door but one up, in my youth. I don't know who had it when I was a child. Ray had half a digit missing; we regularly made all the usual jokes about pies and fingers in them. I trust no one ever ate the missing pointer.

Next came the Chapel (now a "gym" and named, aptly, Heavenly Bodies) and then Owen Street, before some more terraced houses.

In between the two confectioners previously mentioned – Yates's and Taylor's – was a small haberdashery shop owned or run or occupied by my grandmother, Hannah. Grandma assumed the burial position very early she was so laid back. Knitting and silence filled her working days. The shop was full of little boxes and drawers; with paraphernalia so shiny as to make a magpie's eyes glitter. Gran's enthusiasm didn't make the walls bulge or overwork her pulse to any discernible extent. I have no idea what became of the enterprise; it could have all floated away in a sea of serenity so far as I know.

John Chapman sold newspapers in the village. His were the next premises after a single house. He also sold fountain pens of good quality, on display in a bullet-proof (child-proof) cabinet, the front and sides of which were glass with a solid back panel. The display was on top of a display cabinet, making the height some six feet or more. He used to float out from behind the cabinets like an apparition. His opening gambit was always the same "Wa dust want?" If he didn't have that which was requested, he would rest his arm on the counter and consulting his Awkert Bugger's Book of Quotations would offer, "Wi dunt get much call fer them". As he walked away he'd say "Tha might get 'em at Catterall's (newsagents at Watersheddings) when tha goes ta buy thi papers." (The irony was wasted on me at that age. It raises a smile each time I think about it these days.) He vanished as quickly as he had appeared, scratching his head under his flat cap before plopping it back in place again. He seemed totally uninterested.

Lack of interest must have been a paying game for Mr Chapman. He owned the first pale-paint-and-yards-of-chromium-plate car in the village, a pastel blue Zephyr Six, Mark 1. It was parked in the entry next to his shop and on a sunny morning was so shiny it screamed.

He sold Lion ink to those of us who wouldn't use the school's sludgy ink in our fountain pens. The ink was bluey black in a fairly utilitarian bottle. He also sold Waterman's ink; purply royal blue is the only way I can describe the colour, much desired by us all, but expensive and obtainable only by the few. Its greatest asset, however, was the art-deco style bottle it came in. Having one of those perched on your desk, complete with ink, was akin to acquiring a Ferrari when your usual transport was a second-hand pick-up truck. It never happened to me, but I still hope for the Ferrari.

Mrs Bastow's across the passageway was a "mixed" shop but mainly vegetables and tinned food and toffee and chocolate bars and small bags of pre-packed sweets. She sold "Mentho(mental)-Eucalyptus toffees, Fisherman's Friends and Victory V tablets. "Lozenges" the label on the box called the tablets. They tasted like curried cardboard. Believe me, they were disgusting! So we bought them by the ton. Who knows why kids spend money on such stuff except that they were "winter warmers". Your feet were freezing your mouth was hot. Not exactly central heating then.

The entrance to the shop was similar to my idea of entering a prison, alarms and buzzers all over the place. The two outer doors led to a yard-square vestibule with a sprung wooden floor, which caused a buzzer to sound in the shop when receiving your weight. The next obstacles were two more doors with a bell on a spring above them,

71

which clanged when the door opened. You fell into the shop in a daze with your ears and nerves jangling. Mrs Bastow was elderly and slow; this was her early warning system. Even with this technology she still couldn't make it into the shop before her customers, but there was a strategically-placed mirror between shop and living quarters. There was also a middle-aged son who didn't suffer from any debility that I could see.

The Lord helps those who help themselves, but not to sweets from Bastow's shelves.

Bastow's and Eddie Tett's were semi-detached. The latter was appropriately named (heady!) because he was the village barber. A "hairdresser" was unheard of in the 1950s. I can imagine what my mates would have said if I was "going to the hairdresser's".

It would be unprintable. Eddie gave the best value for money in the village. He always, but always, asked, "Short back and sides is it?" as if there was anything else. It cost sixpence and you had to divulge your weekly doings so that he could tell the next customer what you'd been up to.

For the sixpence he threw in some peculiarly coloured hair-cream, which was in a bottle, the same bottle for ten years to my knowledge, and it plastered down any hairs that protested at their treatment. The style was similar to that the youth of today sports and now costs a week's wages. He was a nice chap Mr Tett, with an easy smile and a good line in chat.

Those who didn't frequent Eddie's usually had a basin cut performed by some humourless member of the family. The basin was placed upon the head and used as a template, the hair being cut around it. Any hair that showed below the basin was unceremoniously removed. There was the same social stigma attached to the basin cut as there was to wearing Wellingtons permanently, because you were too poor to afford shoes. The same with those who only washed twice a week.

I don't know if Eddie gained or lost custom after the nit nurse came to school. Immediately after her visit, a few kids turned up wearing a variety of caps; one even wore his father's flat cap. Beneath the headwear would be nothing but a fringe about the length of a small moustache.

Some unhappy individuals carried an extra burden with blotches of iodine about their craniums. This was for ringworm, woodworm, bookworm, some worm or other. These unfortunates were shunned like temperance society supporters, at least until their hair grew back. Our mother rigorously applied the Derbac comb equally to my sister and myself (thank God) and took great delight if she combed out any nit eggs, by popping them with her thumbnail and showing us the results. We were not impressed, mainly because a large chunk of hair would also have been torn from our scalps.

If any lice want to take up residence on my head these days, they will need non-slip feet; the jungle isn't as thick as it was. The tide is lapping up the beach a bit farther than it used to.

I know little about the Moorside Hotel or Tavern as it was known. Except that the two steps at the front entry were quite high, which must have posed problems for those leaving the premises at 11 pm. A bit like stepping off the edge of the world I should think. Still, a few pints of Wilson's anaesthetic would make the stone flags feel like a mattress when collision point came.

Jack Peel the father and Jack Peel the son were in residence. Jack Peel the son was two years my senior and an easygoing lad, until somebody rattled his cage; in the vicinity of Jack was not a good place to be when that happened. Jack was tough.

I vaguely remember that an off licence was attached to the pub; its doorway became a fairly expensive bus shelter where people stood out of the rain awaiting the Denshaw bus.

There was no petrol station or hardware shop in the immediate area of the village when I was a lad. The triangular piece of land now holding these and the bungalow dwellings held the school canteen and this was entered via Grafton Street. The rest of the land lay waste.

I should have mentioned the school canteen earlier in the book because it doubled as a classroom when the population increased, as did the Conservative Club's upstairs room on occasion. In the canteen's case it was home to infant three.

I was a "server" in my final junior year, along with five others; Sid Hatch, Lawrie Turner, PAB, Kay Forrest and Marion Whitlock. I think this was the first team with squad members covering for illness etc. The chief benefits of the occupation were fifteen minutes out of class for hand washing and the walk over, and six blobs of mashed potato each if you could eat them. "Seconds" and second "Seconds" were available if there were any left. "Afters" was a refined name we would not ordinarily use.

We each had an eight- or ten-seater table to attend to. There was a race between us, not with each other but to be back at the serving hatch before the canteen ladies had made up the dinner plates for the next trip to the table. One or two of the seated diners inevitably got gravy down their necks, clothes and in their hair. Carrots and garden peas, sensing freedom, skipped across the table occasionally.

Six teachers at a table removed from the rest sat down on most days, sometimes five. Mr Wrigley sat facing the children and barked commands at those exuberant enough to think school dinners were living high on the hog. We served dinner first to the teachers, in tureens, and stacker plates with aluminium spacers to keep any plated food warm, with gravy boats and trays of hot meats.

Sausages came under the heading of "hot meats".

One episode I clearly remember was of a tin tray full of sausages being unevenly distributed amongst the members of staff. It was one of those delayed reactions from the lad responsible (who shall be nameless, and it wasn't me) one of those hurried occasions when a hot tray, carried by somebody, has gone one step too far from the surface it has been resting on and cannot be returned. Pop Wrigley was not amused to see a beautifully-proportioned sausage sticking up from his cup of tea when the cascade of sausages submitted to the forces of gravity. The next few seconds were taken up with female shrieking while the teacher at first slip was trying to remove a hot sausage from down her blouse. Sausages rolled everywhere like mice seeking the darkness. Hunting them down was accompanied by stifled sniggering and a great deal of satisfaction on my part. It's known as payback time. Mr Wrigley did his impression of an angry buffalo, the lady teacher dabbed at her chest with a hanky, and the perpetrator of the indiscretion had butter rubbed on his blistered fingers. The game ended sausages six, teachers nil, with a goal disallowed for the sausage that was offside. It was so far offside it remained under the far radiator for a number of weeks trying to turn itself into penicillin.

Such is life. On a nice sunny day without rap music and whinging politicians, I can be lulled into thinking we are progressing backwards, you can't get such memories from a computer or such fun from a bag of chips at lunchtime.

At the end of Grafton Street was and is the Post Office. The entrance is squarely across the corner of the building and could claim as its address either the above or Ripponden Road. It chooses the latter.

74

Someone has removed the George V post box from its inserted position mounted in the front wall. Nobody asked if it was alright to replace it with a foul looking obstruction on the pavement, and no-one asked anyone if it was alright to fill the resultant hole in the wall with bright shiny new bricks. It looked like a rash on an elephant's backside. The wall has been "fixed" since and no trace of the box's existence remains.

Alright, the increase in the village population meant that the wall-mounted post-box was inadequate for the increase in mail. However, removing something that had to be painted over regularly because various children wanted to mark their passing with an inscription, has denied hours of tongue-protruding pleasure to later generations of name-gougers.

I should think the ghost of old George was incandescent, tearing around Westminster Abbey, after the removal of one of his last mailboxes. He might have said, "The cheek of it! After all the trouble of putting my name on it and then there's the Crown and painting it family red. Huh! Don't know what the world's coming to. They'll be getting rid of the monarchy next. The country's never been the same since Neville Chamberlain got it wrong. Eee! I don't know!"

Inside, the Post Office had the usual country-store type merchandise, sacks of foodstuffs on the floor, beans, lentils, the predominant smell coming from sacks of potatoes.

The sacks had a variety of metal scoops on top, brass and tin in different sizes. The Postmaster, Harry Wrigley, husband of Winnie and not directly related to Pop Wrigley the teacher, was a pleasant chap. He offered a grocery delivery service, which my mother and father utilised until my father found a grocer's shop in Curzon Street, Oldham, whereupon he announced it was "half the price of Harry's", and that was that. Father dropped his list at Maypole in the said street on his way to work at Seddons (a bit of a detour to Higginshaw you might suppose) and collected the box of groceries on his way home. He balanced the box on the petrol tank of his motorbike, with a system of ropes and knots that would shame an alpine climber, the last loop going around his neck. Pretty innovative stuff eh! Especially if you like soggy biscuits and sugar like melting slush when it has rained *en route*.

Harry's grocery was the principal contender in the retail tug-of-trade with the Co-op, primarily I suspect because people bought groceries there whilst in the shop on Post Office business.

After fighting your way to the counter between suspended scales and sacks, you were confronted by a bank of small wooden drawers each about eight inches square, with mystifying codes taped to the front. They probably held differently priced postal orders, and such like. The prospect of un-sprung mousetraps, things that bite, and someone grabbing your fingers provided amusement while Mr Wrigley was rummaging in the drawers. Shopkeepers (male) wore buff-coloured, thigh-length overall jackets in those days, which made them difficult to spot (if they didn't move that is) among the sacks of spuds.

The centres of both stone steps outside were well worn and could accommodate a large posterior with ease. It was a favourite "waiting" place for kids, friends or enemies; a quick shuffle either way along the step and you were hidden from both approaches. Mrs Wrigley was a bit more tolerant out of the classroom and could raise a smile now and again, behind the counter. The smile on the face of the tiger?

Nah! I've been reading too many Steven King books.

Number 747 Ripponden Road was the "Top Shop". It was at the other end of the "long row" as it was known, next to the backs of Sholver Lane houses. In my time it was renowned for its homemade, penny, iced lollipops – three good sucks and most of the Vimto was gone, leaving a stick full of ice. We used the shop mainly on Fridays because that was delivery day for packets of broken crisps. Ordinary crisps cost three pennies; broken crisp or bits, one penny. The bits were probably sweepings up from the manufacturers. They came in packets, which had so much oil or grease in them, that the ink on the packet ran, blurring the writing. Not that anyone would want to claim the distinction of making them. If you were lucky, there would be salt in a twist of blue paper inside. Some of the bits took some chomping and were, I always suspected, grit and cinder. Still, they all went down Cholesterol Boulevard just the same. The "foodie" Freuds of today would have had the manufacturers locked up and the keys sent to the farthest satellite from Earth. Egon Ronay would have taken up fishing and the Environmental Health Department (food section) would have had a collective fit. Heaven for the price of a penny!

At Strinesdale were two shops, one an asbestos sheet and corrugated roof affair with a box wagon attached to the back for storing merchandise. Six customers and the place was full. The shop changed hands once in my time, the first owner living at the house on the corner of Turf Pit Lane and Whitehall Lane, a council-owned dwelling. The shop was situated at the bottom of Barrowdale Avenue (now Broadstone Avenue). I've no idea what brought about its demise. It always looked as if a good strong wind could remove the whole thing and deposit it at Bishop's Park, Grains Bar. The front bit was on low brick columns, too low to squirm under. There must have been more footballs, tennis balls and other round objects under there than Slazenger make in a year's production. The box bit was on high wheels. I suppose it could have been one of the old, wooden, horse-drawn vans used by the railway parcel service. A permanent, brick-built shop was erected at the bottom of Strinesdale Close (now Hayfield Close).

Opposite the shop and to the rear of number 14 Whitehall Lane are, or were, three old stone houses, known as "Conny Castle". At the turn of the last century one of the houses functioned as "The Conny Castle Temperance Hotel" and had a recreational area with swings and other amusements at the rear, long gone now of course. My mother remembers them, I don't. The only memory I have is of a chap named Bill Sutton living in one of them. I still see him walking along Lees Road regularly. Mrs Buckley's or "Molly's" was the other shop on Roebuck Lane, leading towards Highmoor from Strinesdale. It was a general-purpose shop on a lesser scale than the other; how it managed to keep going I don't know. I think it had an off licence at one time or another; I could be wrong, not being into alcoholic consumption at the time.

The only other shop we gave patronage to was the sweets and ice-cream shop at Grains Bar, now a domestic dwelling, in the small row approaching the Bull's Head or Top Bull. In summer, we were given bus fare and golf money to go and irritate the attendant at the nine-hole pitch and putt course opposite the shop. Walking to Grains Bar saved the bus company the trouble of counting our money, and the shop and ourselves benefited in a more acceptable manner.

A round of golf cost one shilling, for which you got a metal driver, a metal putter and a golf ball with more slices out of it than a lattice pie. The man in charge idled his time away in a green, sentry-box type hut and manifested himself only as a deep, disembodied voice and a hand that gave you your tackle and took your money. There was no one attached to the hand at this stage. "Don't dig any holes and only go round once," came from the inner sanctum. Some hopes he had. Twice round was par for the course so to speak. Tongue-biting concentration and golf balls are not compatible bedfellows and soon all the golf balls would be lost.

The penalty for losing a golf ball was financially debilitating. The toffee shop had already relieved us of our spare money and gone on holiday on the strength of it. The thought that my parents might be presented with a bill for the loss of the balls wasn't a happy one. The solution seemed to be to return the clubs in hammer-throwing style. This we did by launching them in beautiful, spinning, high parabolas, in the general direction of the disembodied one's hut. The man had a wonderful vocal range. The deep basso profundo, which was so nice when we began, became a high treble scream and produced a person hitherto unseen. He performed a kind of rant on the spot, jumping up and down uttering flowery expletives not of a Sunday nature. This created the need to run away. I don't know about anyone else but in my "running away" experiences, an un-scalable wall or a gate with too many cross-members always appears to bar the way. Having got myself into a gasping-for-breath, rhythmic, easy lope, I could rely on my legs to play traitor by becoming rubbery, if the chap was persistent enough my uppermost and all-consuming thought was that if caught I would get killed, a euphemism of the day for a good hiding. This usually provided the killer sprint to freedom. We were quite brave once out of reach, quoting him poems from Keats, lines from Homer's *Iliad*, any of the Ten Commandments and stuff like that. Only later in life did I acquire the knack of first finding an exit before entering anywhere dangerous. Under the "lost ball" circumstances, we could only play once a year even though we were never caught.

Bicycles

Nowadays a new bicycle is what every child gets along with its breakfast or in exchange for a word probably first promoted by the children's retail outlets – "canayav". To own a bicycle was regarded as a real necessity in my formative years. The pleasure of possessing a gleaming, many-geared, world-renowned racing machine was image building and pinpointed your position in the two-wheeled hierarchy. Unfortunately, most of us started off with beaten-up, paint-bereft contraptions, which would frighten today's road safety policemen into early retirement. Very old bikes were usually painted black. The paint could be removed in a number of ways, chief amongst which was by falling from them. Losing a little weight accompanied the practice – the amount of skin I've left on the roads of Moorside would have made a pair of boots. Most of us were well acquainted with the causes of paint removal, some of the finer examples being the unseen brick in the road, the feet on handlebars routine, riding on one side of the bike balanced on the pedal and the bike falling to the other side, waving at someone you've just passed, before a bus hits you, and mounting the bike while it's in motion thereby causing an unstoppable wobble. This practice was known as cocking-on. "Can you cock-on lad?" "Aye! Just watch this."

It was time for the *Elastoplast* a few seconds later.

The most favoured paint remover, the all-time Number One, was the flying dismount, hopping off while the bike was still moving and letting it clatter against the wall. It was the cause of the most terrible anguish and despair if it went irreversibly wrong. Flailing tangles of legs and bike bouncing along the road, dogs running as if the butcher was after them, old ladies gripping their handbags in fear, and the slow painful journey to the doctors. Ah! It was wonderful. I can still feel the laughter rising in me now. Only when it was someone else of course.

Bikes I have seen and in some cases owned have been brakeless, saddle-less, one had odd-sized wheels, and one owned by an older acquaintance had inner tubes but no tyres (for a few seconds anyway).

Audible warning devices were few and far between. Why spend money when a loud "Oiy!" worked just as well? It was desirable to own a bicycle pump in good working order, especially if it was someone else's that you now owned. The possession of a set of lights – either battery-illuminated or dynamo – put you in the executive league. Some kids spent hours fitting cast-off lighting equipment in the full knowledge that they hadn't an ice cube in hell's chance of its working – a bit like fitting the go-faster stripe on a car, hoping it will add 5 mph to its top speed. Long, uninteresting conversations were held, with much sagacious nodding of the head about race pedigree and the cost of extra refinements. I vaguely remember Campagnolo (derailleur gears) and Mafax something-or-other being "wheeled out" as the things to have. Sturmey-Archer, a hub-incorporated gear system, didn't rank much above "fixed" gear, even though it was more readily available than anything else. These conversations usually followed somebody's Christmas bike being given an airing, and were finished by New Year. Excursions were to Norden Lido at Rochdale, which I recall being a red-faced, sweaty do, rigorous because Buckstones Road (long and steep) was at the wrong end of the outing. Blackpool would be talked about enthusiastically under the street lamps at night and studiously ignored in the cold light of day. I know that Terry and Lawrie my mates, at the age of fifteen, set out for Derby on their bikes to see some girls they met while we were on holiday at Middleton Towers. Whether they arrived or not, I don't know. I know darkness came and they didn't. Certain actions had to be performed to impress girls. One was grabbing a lamppost in passing and letting the bike carry on without you, another was hanging onto a bus handrail until the conductor saw you. Riding your bike along a plank supported by bricks and landing in a lorry-load of sand was popular if painful, the bike coming to a dead stop and you not.

Riding through puddles had its moments. Grafton Street was unmade at the time and sported a number of cavities of varying depths. Lifting your feet off the pedals there was a bit of a lottery. Sometimes you kept your feet dry, at others, the whole caboodle, including you, would end up in the water.

On such occasions, I discovered that kicking the bike didn't help. Some of the holes were so deep that with a little imagination you could hear the Agecroft Colliery miners singing below. We spent a lot of time mending punctures, or if you should choose not to repair the tube, the bike could be unceremoniously flung into the shed and not used for months. The thought has often struck me that some stubborn inner tubes resisted the attempt at inflation and that certain well-rounded friends were inflated by default. As long as the pedal pushing roughly coincided with the wheels going round, I don't think anything else really mattered.

Beyond the Village

Entertainment outside the village came in two forms: the Savoy cinema at Hillstores on Saturday afternoons (which I was funded for) and the rugby ground at Watersheddings (which I wasn't). Because of the relative proximity of the latter to Counthill I, or we, always knew when a match was in progress.

Oldham had a very good side in my childhood, objects of worship being Alan Davies, Frank Pitchford, Ike Southward, Charlie Winslade, Rocky Turner and Don Vines. Players I couldn't worship were Bernard Ganley and Roger Dufty. My Great Aunt Amelia, a fervent supporter, said Bernard wasn't a proper rugby player because he still had his own teeth, and he wasn't much of a stopper! The few times I saw Bernard outside the ground he always had a good-looking lady on his arm.

My great aunt thought the first requirements of a good rugby player were cauliflower ears and a nose that preceded you round corners. As for front row men, these players all came from Workington, according to her. If the Workington team was a few men short in the front row, they went to the pit shaft and shouted down. A hooker (not that kind!) and two props came up and away they went with a full team. Bernard Ganley was as good a place kicker as you could get and Roger Dufty was so fit he could burst at the seams. Because they were such a good side, crowd turnouts, even to night matches, were at maximum. When the team was having a good spell of play during the game, the crowd's roar was so loud you could hear it for miles. "Miles" is exactly what I mean, too. This was our cue to pay them a visit. We used to climb the greyhound track wall and work our way into the "penny rush" stand. It was easy if St Helens or Wigan were playing because even the stewards watched the match instead of us.

Wingers were in fashion at the time. Billy Boston was so fast and powerful he could drag half the opposing defence over the try line with him and Brian Bevan was just the opposite, built like a drain rod, bald and with no teeth, but from a standing start you were wasting your time trying to catch him. Tom van Vollenhoven was also in the same category. When these players came to visit Watersheddings, you couldn't gain turn-stile access after 2.45 pm on Saturdays. After the matches, Watersheddings Street was awash with men like migrating wildebeest, running for buses – of which there would be a dozen or so lined up in Counthill Road.

My other regular pastime was the Savoy picture place. In the 1940s and '50s it enjoyed decent patronage. My parents alternated between going there and to the Hillstores ballroom on Saturday evenings. My support for the cinema only ran to Saturday afternoons and then not every week. The Children's Matinee started about 1 pm and lasted until the Lone Ranger and Tonto had killed everybody in Montana, or Buster Crabbe had flown away in his silver cigar case with sparks falling from its base. Some of the characters in the Crabbe space films could have given the punk movement a run for its money in the face make-up department.

Johnnie Weissmuller sometimes finished off the entertainment in the serialisation of the Tarzan films, usually he was vanishing down a crocodile's throat. Then next Saturday he opened his account by swimming like the clappers away from a painted log being dragged by someone out of shot.

Gene Autrey could be heard singing a song while thundering into the sunset and Pancho Villa's horse (on the odd occasion that the projectionist fell asleep) was well capable of 100 mph. Film speed could be a bit erratic in those days.

Because my mother thought I shouldn't consort with the Barrowshaw kids, I was given money to go upstairs. Some of the kids thought this was "elitism" and said so. Throwing empty ice-cream tubs and crisp packets at them from my lofty perch was eminently satisfying.

Kids lined up along Huddersfield Road and the queue then ran down the side street, on which was a fruit and vegetable warehouse. If it was unattended whilst we were waiting to go in, we passed the time throwing potatoes and rotten cabbages at each other. The chap who worked in the warehouse had a fairly nasty temper and a voice to crack the windows. I reckon he hid himself sometimes just so that he could practise his ear-cuffing technique on unwary kids.

Like everything else, with the advent of television the cinema went out of the window.

Tale of a Runaway Tyre

We are now a nation of reveal-alls, and are dragged screaming into psychoanalysis almost from being born. God seems to have moved to one side, and the planet as a whole has a headache. Lawsuits are advertised on the internet and no longer sold at Burtons. So I think that I can tell of an incident that occurred 47 years ago. It is that the front door to number 4 Haven Lane would be asked to repel boarders in a manner it wasn't designed to do. The incident concerns a bus or lorry tyre (for telling purposes it will be a bus tyre) and the above-mentioned door.

The bus tyre hove into view one day, propelled by the youngest of a brood of boys who lived across the way from our house. When questioned about its origins, by my visiting friend and I, he said he'd found it. Everything was "found" in those days. A vision of a double-decker bus limping along minus a front tyre sprang to mind. The tyre's motion was quite wobbly and it covered the ground in fits and starts primarily because it was bigger than the boy, who as well as being a fervent optimist, had a penchant for filling his pockets with frogs and an admirable reputation for resurrecting bonfires. This last activity involved a lot of eye rubbing, cheek puffing, squatting over embers and a very early start.

After an hour of eye wiping, coughing, vigorous, charcoal-encrusted finger work, Zorro's mask would appear on his face. He could spend a whole day blissfully unaware of his panda-like appearance – at least he could until his mother spotted him.

Trailing the streets with the family bogey (a home-made go-cart without engine) with bucket aboard, while searching for horse muck for the garden, seemed to consume much of his out-of-school time. He was irrepressible. He was also younger than us and the tyre was swiftly confiscated. Once out of stone-throwing or run-after range, he practised his not inconsiderable repertoire of vituperation upon us without effect, the get-you-later attitude being adopted. Why children think (or don't think) they won't be asked to pay later, for indiscretions, is a matter for more able minds than mine. Anyway the turn of events would wipe his slate clean because a calamity of some magnitude was about to follow and thoughts of vengeance would be forgotten.

The bus tyre was rolled along the road past Moorside Cricket Club, and made progress unconcernedly down Turf Pit Lane, with a bit of guidance here and there and advice to the guider. Turf Pit Lane has an incline of perhaps 1 in 8. In those days, to a child's eye, it just appeared steeper than it is. Progress was satisfactory until about halfway down. There was a little less satisfaction by the time the tyre reached Sunfield Avenue and developed a will of its own. In its urge to be released from its shackles, it accelerated. The road surfaces were beautifully flat in those days, not much traffic and a smaller size of aggregate made the surfaces black and shiny. The tyre deviated little from its course, and by now had attained a very impressive speed in its bid for freedom.

The walls of the row of three houses and the butcher's shop were asked (by our collective consciences) to restrain the runaway tyre at the end of Haven Lane. We, the accidental perpetrators of the confrontation were now back-pedalling hurriedly. I can remember being fascinated by the tyre's progress. It was and is, a small cameo from which everything else was excluded. When it sprang into the air like an enraged demon, after it had hit the roadside kerb, the door to number 4 stepped forward and was instantly flattened. In its eagerness to impress anyone watching, the tyre seemed to rebound and the topspin took it on again. Bearing in mind that most terraced houses have a small vestibule, the havoc must have been something to behold. I was terrified. I have no recollection of repercussions. My backside can't remember them if there were any.

The muddy footpath leading to Moorside, via Armitage's farm, to the Bull's Head was used for a while after that. Fear is all-encompassing to a child, a form of amnesia seems to prevail. (Ignore it and it will go away.) The incident was not often mentioned between us because of the severity of the foul deed. I have thought over the years (while rummaging around under the layers of guilt) that the householders may have thought that the wheel fell-off-a-lorry. Using today's terminology with regard to things stolen – the wheel did.

I neglected to say at the beginning that the wheel was still in the tyre, adding some considerable weight to it. I shudder to think what would have happened had any type of vehicle turned into the lane from Ripponden Road.

Local Games

Play is an easily-definable pastime, it's what politicians do with money, teenagers do with "the field", adults do with the system, and children do with time.

We often played a game called Rally-O. It involves a person hunting other persons, seconding them to his team to hunt other persons. It is best played at night in autumn. A good hider could spend a week in Blackpool and return to his hiding place with the game still in progress.

Kick-out-ball was similar in method and self-explanatory, except all the caught "hiders" were released if someone kicked the ball from its chosen spot without being seen by a hunter. You knew, if you returned after a longish absence, that if the ball had gone, the game was over.

Tracking or arrow whip was a hunting game again but with only one quarry, who ran off chalking small arrows on the pavement and some minutes later the pack set off in pursuit following the arrows. The hunted one was either caught because of the speedy pursuit or ran out of chalk. Different coloured chalks were used for different games, resulting in the pavements looking as incomprehensible as a Picasso "daubing". If the arrows started heading for the West Riding of Yorkshire, the pursuers might lose interest, and have a game of football, whereupon some hours later, the hunted one would return in disgruntled fashion having arrowed most of the surrounding districts for nothing. These games ran in yearly cycles and differed little. They ran off never to return with the advent of television.

Some engaged in a more chancy type of game in their "testosterone" years, which had hilarious consequences, painful sometimes. It was a variation on the self-explanatory knock-a-door-run-away, practised by the budding sprinters among us.

The idea was to "borrow" a bobbin of your mother's black cotton, wait until darkness fell, tie the cotton quietly to someone's door knocker then unroll the cotton thread gently until you and it were safely behind a wall. The secret was to hide on the hinges side of the door, gently tug the cotton and when the door was answered the cotton was pulled out of the way. On one occasion, a particular house was held siege for a good ten minutes, with the occupant – a short, bald man – running around the outside of the house and back (it was a semi-detached). Eventually he smelled a rat. Most men who worked wore a leather belt and braces, off-shouldering the braces at home. I knew this event had run its course when he shrugged into his braces, ran the back of his hand over his mouth and spat out. Finding the cotton strand he ran down its length and gave Teddy a good cuffing about the head. Teddy wasn't aware he'd been rumbled until the roof fell in. A number of startled irritators rose in unison and darted off like a covey of pheasant. My part in all this was much less dangerous – the thin sheet of glass known as a bedroom window gave me a grandstand view and for these purposes was bullet proof.

Buses

"Chicken" or "Dare" was played only by kids with no self-preservation instinct. Running across the road in front of moving buses wasn't a recommended activity even though the buses were slow moving. It was the stopping part of old buses that was an unknown quantity; some of the drivers were not inclined to stop anyway, relying on the bus's audible warning device as a means of not running into you. I suspect a lot of teeth gritting and wishing for more speed went on in some of those old bus drivers' cabs, the premise being that you, the flattened one, were at fault and I suppose it was so.

Today phalanxes of lawyers would convince the courts that the reason you had been run over was a genetic one because missing buses ran in the family, or that the driver got out of bed that morning in the wrong frame of mind and already had a conviction against him for not paying his electricity bill.

I can't resist a chuckle, to myself of course, when someone's mum is reported in the newspapers as saying "he's not a bad lad really", "he" being 35 years old, having held up five banks, participated in three ram raids and burned down his local pub because the landlord wouldn't serve him after time. Some parents have views on this kind of episode that are quite astonishing.

Anyway back to old buses and stopping them: having established that it was a difficult task, apart from throwing a rope with an anchor attached, out of the driver's window, in the hope of snagging it on a lamppost. A driver with a large, heavy foot to stamp on the brake pedal was the best you could hope for. Maybe the drivers applied the brakes at say Watersheddings, enabling the buses to stop at Hillstores. Who knows?

In my youth buses played a large part in life and scurried about Oldham in packs. There were so many buses sometimes that they used to queue for one passenger, especially at Walshaw Place terminus, Mumps. At other times ... well everyone knows that story.

Buses were mainly Daimler and Crossley in those days, with a sprinkling of Leylands. Most had crash gear boxes (no syncromesh)

89

which meant that by the time the driver was able to engage another gear after waiting for the engine revs to die down, the bus had lost its momentum. Not good on Ripponden Road under a full load going uphill.

A bus full of workers going home was an experience. All the seats were occupied, people hung from the gangway handstraps and one or two stood on the platform. Any person who wanted to get off at Alva Road and signalled their intention by ringing the bell, created an air of expectancy if the bus was full. Passengers alighting the bus was the easy part, getting the bus under way was something else altogether. Setting off again in first gear was usually accomplished, if the engine radiator wasn't boiling over. Engaging second gear was a hurried, grinding affair. If second gear was engaged the bus usually juddered, loosening the floor fittings and some people's teeth in the process. If not engaged, the bus stopped and the standing passengers did a more than fair imitation of a cornfield in a blustery wind. The seated passengers often had to repel the standing passengers and a bit of wailing occurred if the bus rolled backwards because the brakes were too hot.

I recall one bus driver reversing between the rows of terraced houses opposite Alva Road so he could have a run at it. If a bus broke down, there was usually an empty one not far behind but not always. People used to set off walking to Moorside, and on one occasion when I was with my mother, the empty or spare bus sailed past while we were between stops.

"Blinking" was as strong as mother could utter in the use of invective. "That blinking bus, would you blinking believe it, the blinking thing!" would approximate to what she said.

A few of the bus crews in my school days were man and wife and kept to one route. One couple lived around Watersheddings. The lady was shortish with black curly hair and very red lips. She could give you the right price ticket without your asking and if you weren't making any attempt to get off when you should do, gave you a wake-up call from the platform downstairs. You would look into the convex mirror at the top of the stairs and see a large pair of goldfish eyes staring back at you.

The single-deck buses were "C" buses and known to us as "Strinesdale Flyers". They had narrow sliding windows and if you had a thin face you could tilt your head sideways and push it through the open window and then assume the normal head position. One irate bus driver, distracted by a noisy head sticking out like a bump on a log, sneaked down the side of his bus at the next stop and gave the head a lusty thwack with his shiny, knebbed, corporation cap. The head panicked and in its hurry to retract itself, banged its chin, bit its tongue, scraped its ears and bumped an elbow on the seat in front. It was a bit like pulling out a wine bottle cork. The head came in with a sucking woosh. Nobody could speak about the incident for over a week without breaking into eye-watering, table-slapping laughter. You know the type; you can't breathe, get hiccoughs and finish every wet-eyed bout with the sound, "Eeey-eh" before starting again.

Buses had been a source of amusement for a fair bit of my young life. If I can step out of my childhood for a short while, mainly because amusement is for sharing and given a reasonable amount of imagination or memory you can see the value of the "last bus" home. This was the 11 pm from Henshaw Street to Moorside and I would be approximately 17 years old. These incidents always happened on Saturday nights. The upstairs was roughly half full of lads of my age and the rest of the passengers were "drinkers". The lads had been out with their respective girlfriends to the flicks (pictures) or dancing. There wasn't much drinking-while-courting in the late 'fifties and early 'sixties, probably because the girls didn't want to be leapt upon after three pints of Wilson's mild beer. If they did want to be leapt upon, they never said anything to me about it.

As the bus moved out of town, lads would clamber aboard and sit wherever seating was available. I must have dated town girls mainly, because along with my mate Lawrie, I nearly always got the back seat, much prized because you could see everybody who got on and off. Nobody ever sat downstairs except the blokes incapable of climbing the stairs.

You could tell the lads who had been to the pictures because they had one pink, shiny shoulder to their jacket, with shirt collar to match. They achieved this distinction with the help of a lady's face "improver" known as Max Factor's Pan Stick. Stick it did, to whatever it touched. You could tell to which side of the girl the lad had been sitting, therefore which part of his backside got cramp in it and which side of his neck got the crick.

The rest of the upstairs denizens were older men who had frequented the town-centre hostelries. By and large, they spent their time gazing at the front of the bus trying to read the notice about seating capacities, or staring out of the windows while talking to themselves. Constantly swaying, the bus provoked differing reactions in the "drinkers": sleeping with mouth open, sleeping with snoring or sleeping on the person sitting next to them, sometimes a swift rush to the back and a quick fall down the stairs without touching them in order to be sick in someone's garden. Loud singing of some obscure ballad was commonplace, until the passengers gave a concerted bellow of "shaddup"!

There was an occasional eruption of bodies if a person had gone past his stop and didn't want to walk too far back home.

The most entertaining inebriate was the one who did two paces forward and one backwards trying to reach a seat at the front. Invariably he was full to the gunnels, couldn't find his money for the fare and couldn't close his mouth. When eventually he'd focused upon the conductor, asked him if he were married, asked him if sixpence would take him to Timbuktu, and thrown his change all over the floor, he would start singing "Show me the way to go home". He guaranteed everyone's attention by lighting a fag and coughing until we thought he might die. Then he would say "Ah, that's better!" and lurch around to see if he knew anyone. It didn't matter if he did or didn't, he was going to ramble on anyway.

Returning to my childhood. The bus terminus at Moorside was opposite what is now a car lot. The bus would draw up abreast of the Post Office and then reverse into Grafton Street. Occasionally, this manoeuvre necessitated the use of the footpath if the driver was alone. He would be alone because the bus sometimes stopped at the confectioner's, the conductor queuing for sandwiches or pies, while the driver carried on to turn the bus around (and set the table). If the conductor were in attendance he would stand on the bus platform at the rear while the bus backed round, wafting his hand in the general direction of the driver and shouting an extract from the vehicle-reversing manual most frequently used by bus crew, lorry drivers' mates, and all warehouse men. It went along the lines of, C'mon! c'mon! c'mon!, whoa!, c'mon a bit, whoa! Whoa! Whoa! WHOA! Oops. The driver would dismount as if he'd been ejected, to find bits of his bus and slivers of Post Office wall lying around in catastrophic splendour, while the conductor sat on the kerb, head in hands, contemplating the length of the dole queues and wondering why the driver was such a deaf sod. I witnessed one incident where the conductor was a little on the short side, and the driver totally ignored or was unable to see his signalling. Taking matters into his own hands he ended up almost on Mrs Wood's front flags on the corner of Dickens Street. I think his foot may have slipped from the clutch pedal. Much gibbering and "bloody helling" came from the conductor, who by now was half way up the inside of the bus. To my knowledge no member of the public ever got rolled-out but I suspect it was more by good luck than good judgement. Buses waited alongside Mellodew's wall on Ripponden Road for the evening exodus of workers; half-a-dozen double-deckers, sometimes more. If you multiply that by every factory in Oldham and surrounding areas, well, you wouldn't like the fuel bill dropping through your letterbox. If the buses arrived early all the crews would sit on one bus talking, which was an excuse for us to run around the other buses ringing the bells and generally making a nuisance of ourselves.

The only thing you must not do, on pain of a good rollicking, was put your uncollected fare in the little, padlocked, honesty box on the bus platform. We used to withhold our fare if we could until we were getting off the bus, because to us it was a moneybox and we were being honest. Children didn't know about conductors not doing their job properly, or so it would appear to the bus company. Hence the eye-popping scream, as your money tinkled in the bottom of the box. You might, if you were impressionable, be tempted to think that honesty doesn't pay, if you'll pardon the pun.

"Dropping off" the bus was much practised by some and was a considerable health risk. This recreational skill was utilised by certain people as an act of bravado or simply to save their legs from walking back from their bus stop. The method was to stand on the platform holding the handrail, lean backwards calculating the speed and let go, running before you hit the ground.

"Hit the ground" has many meanings. You could be ambling along enjoying some childlike fantasy when the rapid splatter of footsteps as a bus turned a corner intruded into your little world. On special occasions, you would hear the splatter of a body windmilling its way down the road, to land in an undignified heap of raincoat tails, dislodged trilby and ashen countenance. Didn't get that one right then, Mr Whoever!

There are times when the brain doesn't register speed correctly. A bit like the speed camera and your 150 mph, very expensive, Italian sports coupé, I suppose. There was a bench on the corner of Turf Pit Lane, where dropees could apply their brakes, or deposit their hurtling bodies rather than damage Mellodew's foot-thick, high, stone wall.

Imagine sitting there in your dotage when fourteen stones of unco-ordinated miscalculation landed in your lap. The graveyard at St Thomas's isn't big enough for too many mistakes of that nature.

Bear in mind that lamp-posts, particularly the concrete one outside our chippy, might hinder your progress in this dangerous pursuit. Whole columns of vehicles following behind waited for an excuse to gobble up connoisseurs of the art who blundered. The science was widespread.

The top of George Street, Oldham, the bottom of Henshaw Street, and the Star Inn, were all good places to "Drop off".

The Short Arm of the Law

The local constabulary wasn't a looming presence in those days, much like today you could say. Our bobby was a chap named Reggie Hill who lived at Watersheddings. He was a fair-minded but stern man, who was on top of his job, when he wasn't on top of us. I can only remember him having one fit of pique and I don't remember the recipient of this aberration. The outcome of the incident in Turf Pit Lane was the swift swing of his shoulder cape, which connected with the unfortunate's head, or rather the chain, which served as a neck fastener, did. It was a gunfighter thing, wham, bam, ouch! It's odd that in those days no-one ran home and "reported" him for assault, the fact being that you would be likely to get another hiding for being "lippy" to a policeman.

When Reggie was tired or needed some exercise, he put the Constabulary transport to good use. Constabulary bicycles were black, with straight handlebars that bent towards the rider at each end and had lever and rod brakes (no cables). Mudguards were pressed metal, and the saddles were made from something pre-historic. Hard leather for some reason was thought to be the best seating material available. The gear facilities were provided by Sturmey-Archer and numbered three, if the bikes had any gears at all. Roads being what they were, mudguard, chain and probably teeth rattling were commonplace. It was prudent to have a quick glance behind you to see if the aforementioned ensemble was making progress – well anywhere within earshot really.

You can imagine a policeman's eager anticipation when the powers-that-be told him that he was to receive a new two-wheeled vehicle. Much punching of the air and running round the police station with his shirt pulled over his head I'll bet.

Of course, with a little teeth gritting and swift pedalling, arriving at the next "scene of crime" would be speedily achieved as well.

I can't imagine who would be supposed to answer his police whistle if he was in danger. The nearest constable would be about a mile away at Hillstores or Derker. The thought of the Borough's policemen stopping their activities and standing like pointer dogs, cupping an ear and muttering "there goes Reggie Hill's whistle again" would be comforting to him I'm sure, if someone was assaulting Moorside Post Office or himself for that matter. It is a fact that somehow or other, local bobbies always came up with a culprit for misdemeanours. Local knowledge would be an advantage unavailable to today's centralised Constabulary. It is much more likely however that they were able to acquire information about the perpetrators of crimes from knowing the address of a damn good snitch.

There was a resident policeman at Strinesdale, one William Webster (Bill to his adversaries) a very big man with blond hair and moustache. He marched when perambulating, his facial expression one of anticipation, swinging his arms like a Royal Marine drill sergeant spotting his favourite piece of *fairy cake* with a button undone. I fancy he was a southerner, with an ear well-tuned to the grapevine, and not disposed towards the erstwhile art of ear-cuffing. He much preferred to be sitting waiting in your home when you returned to it at teatime. In that way he was able to watch the pain being administered without the indignity of having to chase you. The look on a culprit's face when he saw Bill sitting in their living room, must have given him immense satisfaction.

On the estate was a police box, a Constabulary blue construction, about five feet tall, shaped like a thickset gas lamp, made from cast-iron, and locked. Townfield Police Station was a couple of miles away so the powers-that-be gave him a direct line, albeit half-a-mile from his home. I'm not sure if it was also for public use in emergencies. Bill could be seen reporting in regularly, he was probably ordering lunch as well, assuming he had paperwork to do. Most of a policeman's paperwork was confined to his little black book, whereas today all policepersons have their own computer and are duty bound to produce 300 yards of print each day or they are considered not to be doing their jobs properly. I suppose it gives the criminals a bit more time to go about their chosen activities as well.

My father knew Reggie Hill very well, and spoke at length with Bill Webster about the War. He also knew Walter Alcock (who doesn't in Oldham?) ex-policeman retired court usher and thoroughly good bloke.

Because of my father's reticence I used to wonder which side of the fence he knew them from. I prefer to think it was a keep-well-in-with thing. I may be doing him and them an injustice, however.

Before the advent of the aspiring classes, a PC was a police constable, now it's "personal computer", "politically-correct", and "prawn cassoulet". There are so many abbreviations these days that it seems to me to be a guessing game or a secret language from the Americans.

My world changed with my school and became the town rather than the village.

A Moorside Lad

Wi lived in Counthill Fowt ya know,
Down Haven Lane ta school wi'd go.
Bi t' riding school, past th'owd mill,
Kickin' stones, me an Bill
Mi pal.

Walked in t'schoolyard inta lines.
Shufflin', talked wi' finger signs.
Teacher, stood at front, 'ud shout,
"No talking or you'll get a clout."
Same in t'classroom, never talk,
For, 'e'd think nowt a'chuckin' chalk.
Or t'board duster.

In them days, most wore clogs;
In t'snow, thi made big cloggy-bogs.
Mine 'ad irons, some 'ad rubbers,
Them wi' boots were lucky buggers.
Pants in length wer down ta t'knee.
An' patched
Odd colours.
Nowt wer free.
On'y advice.

About that time, a 'ad a bike.
Fow! tha's never seen the like.
Solid wheels, big at front,
Peddlin' it, thi growth 'ud stunt.
A fancied one wi' spokes an' tyres.
A leather seat ya moved wi' pliers.
Yellow, wi' a chain an' bell,
Could see mysel' goin' like 'ell.

A spent school 'olidays in t'mill,
Thi let mi' wander round at will.
'Cept th' engine house,
That wer all brass an' shiny.
Favverd a ship.

Went past ring room wi' its spinners,
Past blowing room, ta canteen dinners.
After t'sweet, off a'd dodge,
Go an chuck stones inta t'lodge,
Er went ta spend mi pennies.
Ya could stretch a penny far.
Broken crisps, and Arrer bar.
A two-ounce bag a' jelly babies.
Served by grey-haired, aproned ladies.
There wer a bell in t'floor, that rang.

Early morn', wi'd be on t'cart.
Fetchin' t'cotton, off wi'd start.
Down ta t'docks a think wi went,
Two black shires in th' 'arness bent,
Made a' brass, an' well-oiled leather,
Mind, a didn't go if wi'd bad weather.
A stopped behind in t'fire-hole.
Stoker, dusty, shovelled coal.
A number tens t'shovel wer,
Thi 'ad ta bi t'right temperature,
Did t'boilers,
Three on 'em, big uns, Lancashires.
Thi used two, an' flued t'other,
When it 'ad gone cowd.

When t'siren went, wi all went home.
A used ta wander on behind.
Don't think owt wer on mi mind.
Just buggered, a reckon.

In our 'ouse, one down, one up,
It took some time ta get a cup
A tea, ya see,
Wi boiled water on t'fire.
Wi'd gas lights, wi' mantles,
An' when they popped, thi made mi jump.
A must a stopped
Mi 'eart, some-an-oft'.
Wi'd fly papers an' DDT,
An' dolly blues, an owd settee,
It wer imitation leather,
Cowd ta t'legs, an' owt whatever touched it.
An owd slop-stone, it weren't 'alf shalla',
An' leather things ya rubbed wi' talla',
Clogs an such.
Coconut mattin', laid on t'floor,
A knob an' latch, on t'pantry door.
Come ta think wi wer poor,
There's no two ways about it.

Sunlight through t'front windas shone.
Some 'ad lead, an' some 'ad none.
T'toilet wer a way o'er yon',
An' everybody knew ya'd gone,
An' when ya came back too.

Thi wun't put up wi' that taday,
Thi wern't good days a 'ave ta say,
Still, a wer on'y a lad i' play,
After t'War.

© David J. Lavisher. 2002